THE

FINANCIAL

WRITER'S

Stylebook

Also by Chris Roush

"A Century of Progress: Celebrating Progress Energy's History of Service"

"A Good Night's Sleep: The Pacific Coast Feather Story"

"Inside Home Depot: How One Company Revolutionized an Industry"

"Profits and Losses: Business Journalism and Its Role in Society"

"Show Me the Money: Writing Business and Economics Stories for Mass Communication"

THE
FINANCIAL
WRITER'S
Stylebook

1,100 BUSINESS TERMS
DEFINED AND RATED

CHRIS ROUSH AND
BILL CLOUD

Marion Street Press
Portland, Oregon

Published by Marion Street Press
4207 S.E. Woodstock Blvd. # 168
Portland, Ore. 97206-6267
USA
http://www.marionstreetpress.com/

Subscribe to the book online at http://www.fiwords.com/

Orders and desk copies: 800-888-4741

Printed in the United States of America

ISBN 978-1-933338-38-5

Cover Art Direction by Nicky Ip

Library of Congress Cataloging-in-Publication Data
Roush, Chris.
  The financial writer's stylebook : 1,100 business terms defined and rated / by Chris Roush and Bill Cloud.
      p. cm.
  Includes bibliographical references.
  ISBN 978-1-933338-81-1
  1. Journalism, Commercial—Style manuals. 2. Journalism, Commercial—Terminology. 3. English language—United States—Usage—Dictionaries. I. Cloud, Bill. II. Title.
  PN4784.C7.R65 2011
  808'.06665--dc22
                                    2010036313

CONTENTS

ACKNOWLEDGMENTS

As with any book, credit must be given to those behind the scenes.

This stylebook is the product of a number of people besides the authors. Allan Sloan, the current Fortune magazine senior editor at large and perhaps the best business journalist out there today, gave invaluable guidance early on and then read the entire manuscript — twice — to give feedback.

Herb Greenberg, a former business columnist for Marketwatch.com, TheStreet.com, The San Francisco Chronicle and others who is now with CNBC, also provided feedback, as did Adam Levy, a former business journalist, former Loeb Award winner, former Wall Street analyst and friend.

The legal section at the end of the book could not have been compiled without the help of Michael Hoefges, an attorney who teaches mass communication law at the University of North Carolina at Chapel Hill, and two Dow Jones & Co. attorneys — Mark Jackson and Jason Conti. The accounting and financial definitions were reviewed by Ed Maydew, the David E. Hoffman Distinguished Professor of Accounting at the University of North Carolina at Chapel Hill.

I also gave versions of the stylebook to several business journalists — and some college students who want to be business journalists — and asked for their opinions. Those who gave me feedback were Bloomberg reporters Amy Thomson and Sapna Maheshwari, and former students Sarah Frier and Andrew Dunn.

I look at this stylebook as a work in progress. While it's something that I wish I had while working as a business reporter, it will get even better in the future. Don't hesitate to let us know how we can add to or fine-tune the entries.

— Chris Roush, University of North Carolina at Chapel Hill

FOREWORD

Business has its own language. Unfortunately, it's not English. It's what I call bizspeak, a pseudo-language full of terms and shorthand and buzzwords that none but the initiated understand. And even many of the initiated can't explain to the uninitiated what these terms mean.

This stylebook helps you translate bizspeak into English, both for yourself and for your audience. Think of it as a foreign language guide, and also as a reminder that even though you may now understand the term after reading about it, much of your audience probably doesn't.

So make sure to use as much English and as little bizspeak as you can. That way, you're serving the initiated and uninitiated alike.

Many of the words that we business journalists use and understand — or think we understand — are, in fact, euphemisms that we'd do well to avoid. My favorite: "correction," used to describe a big decline in prices of stocks or houses or some other asset. If the new, lower prices are in fact correct, which is what "correction" implies, did we call the price rise preceding the decline a "mistake"? Obviously not. Use words that convey substance, not spin.

This book also gives you an objective reason to avoid using the absurd exclamation marks that the likes of Yahoo and Yum Brands insist are part of their names. So if Yahoo folk want to know why you didn't call them Yahoo! folk, invoke the stylebook.

Unlike other stylebooks I've seen during my 40 years in business journalism, this one isn't written for a particular organization. It's written for all of us. A feature I especially like is that the book recognizes that business audiences, general audiences and trade audiences are different from each other, and makes allowances for those differences.

This book isn't perfect — what is? But even if, like me, you don't agree with all the definitions and second-use suggestions here, that's small beer. The book is an invaluable guide to helping you get business right, understand it and explain it. Which is, of course, what we all should be trying to do.

— Allan Sloan, senior editor at large, Fortune magazine

INTRODUCTION

I once got into a debate with a reporter who had written that natural gas was selling at $2.50 (as I recall) per million cubic feet. I didn't know much about commodity pricing, but a million cubic feet of anything, I argued, would cost more than that. The figure's right, the reporter replied, because the figure was listed as "mcf" and his source told him what it meant. Thankfully, a reporter experienced in the market settled the argument: The "m" represented 1,000, as in a Roman numeral. The gas was priced per 1,000 cubic feet.

What I needed then, and what both editors and writers need now, was access to this manual. It's a quick way to decode a business term and get guidance on how to use the term in a story. I could have shown the entry to the reporter, and both of us could have quickly gotten back to work. (The manual also would have saved me embarrassment on the many times I've raised similar questions and turned out to be wrong.)

Sadly, as media organizations downsize, there are fewer experienced business writers and even fewer specialized business copy editors. But at least with this manual, there is more help for those still on, or new to, the job.

What you'll find in these pages are explanations for more than 1,100 terms that might pop up in corporate documents, regulatory filings and government reports, as well as phrases that come out of the mouths of corporate CEOs and press representatives. We'll tell you what the terms mean, when they should or shouldn't be used and defined for readers (check our rating system) and how to use them. Some will be fun to know even if they should never appear in print.

It gives guidance on what all those abbreviations (APR, CUSIP, LLC, TARP) mean and when they are acceptable. There's a section devoted to the rapidly growing and changing list of technology terms. And it provides an up-to-date roll call of tricky company names and trademarks as well and guidance on their punctuation and capitalization.

As the business world grows and changes, this book will grow and change as well. Starting in 2011 you'll also have the option to subscribe to a continually updated online version of the text at our website, fiwords.com. And you'll be able to help us keep our list updated and improve the next print edition as well. Contact us at Campus Box 3365, University of North Carolina at Chapel Hill, Chapel Hill, NC 27599-3365 or send us an e-mail at croush@email.unc.edu and bcloud@email.unc.edu with your ideas.

But keep this print edition handy. You'll find it will improve your reporting, speed up your editing and let you avoid overly long discussions on what mcf means.

— Bill Cloud, University of North Carolina at Chapel Hill

LISTINGS KEY

Here is a typical entry for this stylebook:

> **buyback (n.), buy back (v.)** The repurchasing of shares by a company to decrease its number of shares outstanding. A company *will buy back* those shares. Just because a company announces a buyback plan doesn't mean that the shares will actually be repurchased. Some companies will announce a buyback plan to support its stock price, but not actually repurchase the shares. Also, a company may buy back its stock to inflate its **earnings per share** number. Earnings per share is net income available for common stock divided by total number of shares outstanding. With fewer shares outstanding, the EPS number may rise. The term *share repurchase* is also acceptable. **($$)**

The **bold word** or **words** at the beginning of an entry illustrate the accepted usage. An acceptable abbreviation of the word or phrase might be included at the end of an entry. Unacceptable abbreviations are also mentioned when necessary.

If the part of speech is necessary to distinguish usage, it will be indicated in parentheses after the word.

The dollar signs in parentheses after the entry are used to provide a guideline on when the word or term should be defined in business journalism. See p. 16 for the stylebook's rating system.

Italicized words in an entry show how the term can be used in writing or show similar acceptable terms.

Bold words in an entry can refer to another entry in the stylebook or to a related term.

Every attempt will be made to define the entry and provide an explanation of what it means in the business world.

In some cases, an entry might provide tips on how to use it in reporting or writing. For example:

earnings story guidelines: Nearly every business journalist at some time will write a story about a public company's earnings. Some will even write a story about a private company's results. The following guidelines are important to consider in such stories:

- When calculating the earnings growth or decline, focus on the net income or net loss, not the earnings per share. Companies can manipulate their earnings per share growth by decreasing the number of shares outstanding through share repurchase programs.

- Leads need to emphasize why a company's earnings rose or fell during the quarter. Don't just tell the reader that the earnings rose or fell by a certain percentage. They'll want to know the reason.

- Context, context, context. If a company's earnings have fallen after quarters of increases, then you'll need to tell the reader the last quarter in which earnings fell. Was there a loss in the quarter? Then tell the reader when the last quarterly loss occurred. Net income rose 49 percent? When was the last quarter that profits rose faster?

- Listen to the conference call. Sometimes, the story is not the press release with the numbers, but what the executives say to the analysts and investors later in the day. One telltale sign is to watch how the stock price reacts while you're listening to the call. If the price begins to move up or down dramatically, then something newsworthy was said.

- Compare a company's quarterly earnings with the same quarter from the previous year, not the previous quarter. Many businesses are cyclical, making the better comparison the same time a year ago. You can't compare, for example, Coke's second-quarter earnings with the first quarter because it's hotter in the second quarter and more people are thirsty.

- When writing about earnings, focus on the most-recent earnings first before mentioning the same quarter a year earlier. For example, write *Earnings rose 25 percent to $4.5 billion from $3.6 billion in the same time period a year ago,* not *Earnings rose 25 percent from $3.6 billion in the time period a year ago to $4.5 billion.*

- Whom are you going to quote? Increasingly, investors in the stock are being quoted in stories about the earnings, not buy-side analysts. While both have a bias, the investors have less of a conflict of interest.

This style guide is not intended to be the business reporter's sole reference when it comes to style. It should be used in conjunction with another stylebook, such as the latest edition of the Associated Press Stylebook and Libel Manual. This stylebook, however, is intended to fill in the many gaps for business journalists when it comes to other reference materials, which historically have downplayed or ignored the special needs required to report and write business news.

If you cannot find an entry in this stylebook, please refer to the AP stylebook or the Webster's New World Dictionary of the American Language. If you are still not satisfied, or don't have an answer to your style question, please drop us a line and we will consider adding an entry in a following edition.

RATING SYSTEM

Many words and phrases in this style guide have dollar signs listed after them.

The dollar signs, based on a five-level scale, make it easy for a business journalist to decide whether the term or phrase needs defining for his of her audience.

A term or phrase with no dollar sign next to it means that it does not need to be defined in any media form. A term or phrase with a **$$$$$** next to it means that it should be defined in all media.

Here is how we've delineated the different levels of this five-point scale:

$ Daily newspaper business page or section.

$$ Weekly business newspapers, such as those operated by Crain Communications and American City Business Journals, as well as trade publications, such as Nation's Restaurant News or Beverage Digest.

$$$ Television networks or shows devoted to business news, such as "Nightly Business Report" on PBS or CNBC and Fox Business Network, as well as websites and blogs that focus on business and financial news, such as TheStreet.com, Marketwatch.com, Moneywatch.com and SeekingAlpha.com.

$$$$ Personal finance publications such as Money, SmartMoney and Kiplinger's Personal Finance, and weekly and semi-weekly business magazines such as Bloomberg Businessweek, Forbes and Fortune.

$$$$$ Daily business newspapers such as The Wall Street Journal, Investor's Business Daily and The Financial Times, as well as publications designed for the hard-core investor, such as Institutional Investor and Bond Buyer.

In other words, if a term or phrase is rated a **$$$$**, and The Wall Street Journal is a **$$$$$**, then every media outlet that falls into a category rated at or below **$$$$** should define the term or phrase, but The Journal need not.

When ranking words and phrases, we've taken into consideration how these are currently being used in business publications, as well as where we think improvements could be made for the benefit of the readers.

BIBLIOGRAPHY

Any business journalist who cares about his or her craft needs to have some, if not all, of the following books. These offer further explanation of topics in this stylebook.

"Bottom Line Writing: Reporting the Sense of Dollars." By Conrad Fink. Ames, Iowa: Iowa State University Press: 2000.

"Covering Business: A Guide to Aggressively Reporting on Commerce and Developing a Powerful Business Beat." By Robert Reed and Glenn Lewin. Oak Park, Ill.: Marion Street Press: 2005.

"Profits and Losses: Business Journalism and its Role in Society." By Chris Roush. Oak Park, Ill.: Marion Street Press: 2006.

"Show Me the Money: Writing Business and Economics Stories for Mass Communication." By Chris Roush. Mahwah, N.J.: Lawrence Erlbaum & Associates: 2004.

"The Bloomberg Way: A Guide for Reporters & Editors." By Matthew Winkler. New York: Bloomberg News: 2009. 11th edition.

"The Economist Style Guide." London: Profile Books: 2005.

"The Wall Street Journal Guide to Business Style and Usage." By Paul R. Martin. New York: Simon & Schuster: 2002.

"The Wall Street Journal Guide to Understanding Money & Investing." By Kenneth M. Morris and Virginia B. Morris. New York: Lightbulb Press: 2004. Third edition.

"Writing About Business: The New Columbia Knight-Bagehot Guide to Economics and Business Journalism." Edited by Terri Thompson. New York: Columbia University Press: 2000.

"Understanding Financial Statements: A Journalist's Guide." By Jay Taparia. Oak Park, Ill.: Marion Street Press: 2003.

I. STYLEBOOK

A&W Restaurants Inc. A subsidiary of Yum Brands Inc. Use the ampersand and the capital W in all references. The restaurants exclusively sell draft A&W Root Beer, though that brand is owned by Cadbury Schweppes PLC.

abbreviations Many companies, such as **GE**, **GM** and **IBM**, are more commonly known by an abbreviation. Some companies, such as **FedEx** and **Alcoa**, are now referred to by a shortened version of their names. Do not abbreviate a company name on first reference unless it is commonly known by its abbreviation. The Associated Press Stylebook says to use IBM on first reference, but GE and GM on second reference only. We agree.

above water Refers to the value of an asset and implies that the value is above its cost. Although being above water is a good thing, avoid this term in writing except in direct quotes because many consumers are unfamiliar with it.

A.C. Moore Arts & Crafts Inc. The Berlin, N.J.-based craft store chain uses the ampersand in all references.

Ace Hardware Corp. Capitalize only the A in the first name of the Oak Brook, Ill.-based hardware store chain.

Ace Ltd. Lowercase the Swiss-based insurance company's name after the A even though it uses all capital letters.

ACNielsen Corp. The New York-based information services company does not use periods in its name, and spells *ACNielsen* as one word. It's best known for its Nielsen television viewer ratings.

accounts payable Amounts owed to suppliers that must be paid off within a short period of time. They are included on a company's balance sheet as a liability. **($$)**

accounts receivable Reflects the amount of goods or services that a company has sold but has yet to receive payment for. These are listed as an asset on a company's balance sheet. **($$)**

accretive An adjective used to describe when a merger, acquisition or stock buyback will add to a company's profits. **($$$)**

accrual accounting The standard accounting method for most companies. It differs from the **cash basis accounting** method by recognizing revenues when earned rather than when received and expenses when incurred rather than when paid. Publicly traded firms are required to use the accrual method per **generally accepted accounting principles**. **($$$)**

across-the-board A term often used to describe the stock market when virtually every sector is seeing increases in stock prices.

acquisition When one company purchases a stake in another company. It can be either a majority or a minority position, although many acquisitions are for 100 percent of the company being sold. When an acquisition is announced, it often has not closed yet, so avoid writing that Company A has acquired a stake in Company B. The story should be written as Company A has agreed to acquire a stake in Company B.

When writing about acquisitions, make sure that the following facts are included in the story:

1. The total price, including debt that the buyer will have the responsibility to pay, which should be in the lead;
2. If stock is part of the purchase, the terms, such as how many shares of stock in company A will be given to shareholders of company B;
3. The reason for the deal;
4. Whether the deal is **accretive** or dilutive;
5. The stock price reaction;
6. A price comparison to other deals in the same industry;
7. Whether there were unusual trading levels in either company before the deal was announced;
8. The investment banks that advised each company.

acquisition indigestion A slang term in which the two companies involved in an acquisition have had trouble integrating their operations. It can also be used to describe a company that has made multiple acquisitions and is now having trouble integrating those businesses. **($$)**

activity A term often attached to a noun, such as manufacturing, market or trading that is redundant.

Adidas AG Capitalize the first letter of the Herzogenaurach, Germany-based sporting goods company even though it lowercases its name.

Aegon N.V. Capitalize only the first letter in the first name of the life insurance company based in The Hague, Netherlands.

adjusted gross income A measure of taxable income for tax purposes. It is your total income minus items such as deductions related to business activities, moving expenses, alimony paid and deductible student loan interest. It should not be confused with **taxable income**, **disposable income** or **discretionary income**. **($$)**

adjustable-rate mortgage A mortgage where the interest rate paid by the consumer fluctuates. It's also known as a *floating-rate mortgage* or a *variable-rate mortgage. ARM* is acceptable on second reference. **($)**

adverse opinion A statement by the auditor about a company's financial statements that the statements do not fairly represent the company's operations. Adverse opinions signal a disagreement between the auditor and the company, and they are typically viewed as a negative for the company. An adverse opinion found in a company's SEC filings is considered a news story. **($$$)**

Aflac Inc. Capitalize only the first letter in the first name of the Columbus, Ga.-based insurance company.

AFL-CIO The American Federation of Labor and Congress of Industrial Organizations. It is the largest union organization in the United States. *AFL-CIO* is acceptable on first reference.

after-hours trading Trading that occurs after the major U.S. markets close at 4 p.m. EST by electronic communication networks, or ECNs. Trading after hours is voluntary, so there may not be a market for all public stocks. Dow Jones Newswires uses the term *after-hours session* to refer to such trading. **($)**

after-tax income The amount of money left over after an individual or a company has paid federal, state and local taxes. For a consumer, this is also called **disposable income. ($)**

Alamo Rent A Car The St. Louis-based company does not hyphenate its name.

Alcoa Inc. *Alcoa* is acceptable on all references to the company formerly named Aluminum Co. of America.

after the bell A term commonly used to describe an event after the market closes. When a company makes an announcement after 4 p.m., it is considered after the bell. Hyphenate before a noun: *an after-the-bell announcement.*

AG See PLC entry.

Aldi Inc. The Essen, Germany-based grocery store chain, which has locations in the United States, should be spelled with lowercase letters after the A, in contrast to the company's all-cap spelling.

allotment A term used to describe the number of shares given to each underwriter of a public offering, either initial or secondary, to sell to its customers. **($$)**

Allstate Corp. Do not use the "the" before Allstate on any reference to the Northbrook, Ill.-based insurance company.

alternative investment An investment other than stocks, bonds and cash. It can be used to describe investments such as commodities, real estate, private equity, **venture capital** and **hedge funds. ($$$)**

Amazon When referring to the online retail company, write Amazon.com Inc. on first reference and Amazon on subsequent references. When referring to its website, write Amazon.com on all references.

AMC Entertainment Holdings Inc. Capitalize the letters AMC in the name of the Kansas City, Mo.-based movie theater chain.

American City Business Journals Inc. The parent company of 40 weekly newspapers across the country. Its headquarters is in Charlotte, N.C. Although commonly used, avoid the abbreviation ACBJ on second reference. *American City* is preferred.

American Depositary Receipt A certificate issued by a bank that represents shares of a foreign company traded on a U.S. stock exchange. All three words are capitalized. *ADR* is acceptable on second reference, but this term should be defined somewhere in the story. Note that the second word is depositary, not depository. **($$$$)**

American International Group Inc. The name of the New York-based insurance company can be abbreviated to *AIG* on second reference.

American Stock Exchange Now formally known as NYSE Amex Equities because the American Stock Exchange was acquired by NYSE Euronext, the parent of the New York Stock Exchange, in October 2008. The American Stock Exchange was once a major competitor to the NYSE. Use *NYSE Amex Equities* on first reference, and either *the Amex* or *the exchange* on second reference.

Amerigroup Corp. Capitalize only the first letter in the first name of the Virginia Beach, Va.-based health insurer. The company uses all capital letters for Amerigroup.

amortization An accounting practice that over time deducts from profits the purchase price of an asset. When a company purchases a new computer mainframe for $30 million, it may amortize the value of that computer over three years. That means the value of that asset decreases by $10 million on its books each year for three years. A company may change its amortization schedule to a longer time period to slow the decline in value of its assets on its books and thus increase its reported profits. Strictly speaking, amortization goes with intangible assets while **depreciation** goes with tangible assets. **($$$$)**

ampersand Use when part of a company's formal name. Otherwise, do not use in place of "and."

AMR Corp. The Fort Worth, Texas-based parent company of American Airlines. Capitalize AMR in all references.

analyst A financial professional who gives opinions about whether investments should be bought or sold. There are two types of analysts. A **sell-side analyst** works for a brokerage and places recommendations such as "buy," "hold" or "sell" on an investment based on his or her research. A **buy-side analyst** works for a mutual fund company or money manager and researches investments for purchase by his or her firm. Both types of analysts typically focus their research on companies in a specific industry, such as banking or retail.

Business journalists commonly quote both. With sell-side analysts, however, it has become increasingly common to disclose whether the analyst owns the stock personally and whether the analyst's firm has done any investment banking business with the company within the past two years. These disclosures are typically found at the end of a sell-side analyst's report. If a reporter doesn't have the report, ask the analyst at the end of the interview.

Once a common source for business journalists, sell-side analysts are now less willing to talk on the record because of these disclosure rules.

Many brokerage firms now require journalists to seek approval from their public relations staff before talking to an analyst.

Note that there are also analysts who work for the rating agencies and evaluate the debt issued by a company. These analysts are considered to have fewer ethical conflicts.

Many companies list the sell-side analysts that follow their stock on their website. A business reporter should ask analysts to put him or her on their distribution lists so that the reporter may receive their reports. Many analysts now distribute research via e-mail.

angel investor An individual who provides start-up money for a new company in exchange for an ownership position. Angel investors typically invest their own money rather than investing money for others. **($$$)**

Anheuser-Busch InBev The St. Louis-based brewery Anheuser-Busch is now part of this company after its 2008 takeover by InBev. The headquarters is in Belgium.

annual meeting A meeting held by a company for its shareholders to vote on matters such as the election of directors, the approval of an **independent auditor,** and outside shareholder proposals. Although annual meetings are not open to the general public, many companies allow business reporters to attend and provide access to company executives either before or after the meeting. (See the annual meeting entry in the "business news legal issues" section at the back of this book.) Annual meetings are also a good place for reporters to meet investors in the company. *Shareholders meeting* is also acceptable.

annual percentage rate The annual interest rate that is charged for borrowing money. A credit card that charges a 1 percent monthly interest rate has a 12 percent annual percentage rate. *APR* is acceptable on second reference. **($)**

annual report A once-a-year publication required of public companies to provide financial and operating information to its shareholders. The report typically begins with a letter from the company's **chief executive officer**. The document sometimes has news in it. The formal annual report is filed with the Securities and Exchange Commission and is the Form 10-K.

annuity A financial product that typically has a variety of investments such as mutual funds for the purchaser to choose from. Ideally, these investments grow in value and provide a stream of income for the holder during retirement. Also, some annuities pay fixed returns for life of the annuitants. **($$)**

anti-takeover measure A tactic by a company's **board of directors** to ward off unwanted acquisition overtures.

antitrust No hyphen. Antitrust refers to government action to prevent a monopoly in an industry. Antitrust laws prohibit monopolistic control of an industry.

appraisal The valuation of a piece of property by an expert in that field. It can be real estate, an antique or an old car. Many appraisers have an official designation from a governing body. If you're writing about an appraisal, ask who did the appraisal and seek their qualifications. **($$)**

Aqua-Lung A trademarked brand name. Note the hyphen and the capitalization. The generic term is underwater breathing apparatus.

Aramark Corp. Capitalize only the first letter in the name of the Philadelphia-based food service provider.

arbitrageur An investor who attempts to profit from inefficiencies in the market by going long and short in assets that have similar characteristics but are trading at different prices. This is known as classic arbitrage. Another kind of arbitrageur, a risk arb, speculates on announced takeovers. An arbitrageur might buy shares of a company making an acquisition and short on the targeted company, hoping to profit both ways if the deal falls through. **($$$$)**

arbitration A hearing regarding a dispute. Many investor disputes with brokerage houses are settled by arbitration. The decision is typically final.

Arthur Andersen A now-defunct accounting firm that was involved in the Enron scandal. Note the "en" at the end of Andersen.

articles of incorporation Documents filed with the government that detail the creation of a corporation. These documents, typically filed with a Secretary of State's Office in a state government, can include information about the corporation's location, owners and officers.

ask (n., adj.) The price that a stock seller is willing to accept for his or her shares. Also called the offering price, although this term should be avoided because it also refers to the price at which shares in an initial public offering are sold. Can be used as a noun as *the ask* or an adjective as *the ask price.* **($$$)**

assessed value The value given to a piece of property such as real estate or a vehicle for assessing taxes.

asset-backed securities Investments that derive their value from an asset, such as mortgages or credit card loans. Theoretically, such assets spread the risk of the investment because the securities are spread among borrowers and the securities

are owned by many investors. Do not use ABS on any reference. **($$$$)**

assets Items that a company or individual owns that have value. **Current assets** include cash and short-term investments, such as stocks. **Fixed assets** include property, machinery and equipment.

asset-turnover ratio The amount of sales generated by a company for every dollar in assets it owns during a certain time period, such as a quarter or a fiscal year. The ratio is calculated by dividing revenue by assets. The higher the number, the better. Companies with low profit margins, such as grocery stores, have high asset-turnover ratios. **($$$$)**

Associated Press Do not capitalize "the" when used before the name.

AstroTurf A trademarked name that is one word. Note the capital T. The generic term is artificial surface.

AT&T Corp. Headquartered in Dallas. *AT&T* is acceptable on second reference. Do not spell out American Telephone & Telegraph in any reference. Its name is now AT&T.

attribution An important issue in any business news story, attribution needs to be specific in some cases to let the reader know where important facts and information came from. Use *according to* when referring to documents such as SEC filings, lawsuits, depositions, contracts, etc. Use *said* or another verb that describes how the person talked when attributing something to a person.

auction A sale to the highest bidder.

audited financial statement Describes a company's financial statements that have been prepared and certified by a **certified public accountant**. The statements must meet generally accepted accounting principles, or GAAP. **($$)**

auditor A person or firm qualified to examine and audit a company's **financial statement**.

auditor's report A short statement by the auditing firm found in a company's SEC filings. It will explain the auditor's responsibilities, the scope of the audit, and the auditor's opinion about the financial statements.

AutoNation Inc. Maintain the capital N in the name of the Fort Lauderdale, Fla.-based auto dealership chain.

Avis Budget Group Inc. The Parsippany, N.J.-based company does not hyphenate the name of subsidiary Avis Rent a Car System LLC.

avoid A rating given to a stock by a sell-side analyst. It is equivalent to a "sell" rating. **($$$)**

Babies R Us A division of Toys R Us. Do not use the single quotation marks around the R.

backdating The practice of placing an earlier date on a document than when the agreement was executed. In recent years, companies have been charged with backdating **stock options** given to executives so that the options are dated when the company's shares were at a lower price than when the options were granted. **($$$$)**

backlog The total value of orders waiting to be filled, typically for a manufacturing company. An increase in the backlog could indicate a company is having trouble keeping up with its orders, or that orders are increasing, or it could signal that the **economy** is improving. **($)**

back-of-the-napkin business model A term used to describe a rough outline of a company's business model. Also common is **back-of-the-envelope business model. ($$)**

back office The administrative and support personnel of a financial services company. These are the employees who are involved in trade-clearing, regulatory compliance and accounting, for example. **($$)**

bad-debt reserve An accounting entry that a company, especially financial institutions, sets up to reflect loans that it has made that might go bad. Also called **loss reserve. ($$$)**

bailout A term used to describe when a business, individual or the government provides funding to a company that might fail without the investment. In most cases, the government bails out a company to protect the economy. It's one word, with no hyphen. **($$)**

Bake-off A trademarked event. Note the hyphen and the lower case o. The generic term is baking contest.

balance sheet A **financial statement** compiled by a company that shows its assets, its liabilities and its shareholder equity. Assets should always equal liabilities plus shareholder equity. On a balance sheet, look to see if a company's **accounts receivable** or **accounts payable** have increased dramatically since the previous balance sheet. That could be a sign that the company is having trouble paying its bills or is having trouble collecting payments.

balloon payment A loan that has a large amount of money due at the end of the loan. Balloon loans are attractive to short-term borrowers because they have a low interest rate. Some balloon loans allow the borrower to reset the interest rate at the end of the term to the current market rate. Do not use as a synonym for an interest-only loan. **($$$$)**

Bancorp Do not use Bancorp as a standalone name. It's a common abbreviation of bank corporation used by banks throughout the country, the largest being U.S. Bancorp.

Band-Aid A trademarked product. Note the hyphen and the capital A. The generic term is adhesive bandage.

bank closure When a bank is closed by federal or state regulators, the Federal Deposit Insurance Corp. sells the branches and the deposits to another bank in the market. No advance notice is given to the public when a financial institution is to be closed. Customers can continue to use their checks, debit cards and the ATMs of the closed bank. A bank closure typically happens on a Friday after the banks have closed for the day, and the banks reopen on Monday under the name of the new bank.

bank holding company Any company that has control over a bank. It is required to register with the Federal Reserve System. Bank holding companies can issue stock with greater regulatory ease than other banks. The largest bank holding company in the country, as of March 31, 2009,

is Bank of America Corp. It had $2.3 trillion in assets on that date. Do not use BHC in any reference. **($)**

Bank of America Corp. The name of the bank company based in Charlotte, N.C. However, its investment banking subsidiary is called Banc of America Securities LLC.

bankruptcy A legal proceeding that occurs when an individual or a business is unable to pay all its debts as they come due. The federal government runs the bankruptcy court system. The bankruptcy court system allows the person or company to reorganize its debt so that it can be paid off. With some bankruptcy filings, part of the debt can be eliminated.

When covering a bankruptcy court case, it's important to obtain the following documents:

- The initial filing, which will list the amount of the assets and the amount of the liabilities of the filer.
- The creditors' list, which will list every individual and business owed money. This list comes with addresses. Consider it a source list.
- The reorganization plan, which will detail how the debtor in a Chapter 11 bankruptcy plans to pay off its debt and emerge from bankruptcy court protection.
- The judge's ruling approving the reorganization plan.

When writing about companies filing for bankruptcy, do not state that the business is closing its doors unless it has filed for Chapter 7 bankruptcy. This is a liquidation. With a Chapter 11 bankruptcy, a company hopes to reorganize its debt and emerge from bankruptcy court as a continuing business. **($$)**

Bankshares, Bancshares Spell as one word if it is spelled that way in a company name.

bargain hunting Avoid this term. One investor's bargain may be expensive to another.

Barron's A weekly business newspaper that is a subsidiary of Dow Jones & Co. Its first edition appeared in 1921, and it is named after former Dow Jones head Clarence Barron. The "Up and Down Wall Street" column is widely read. Note that the apostrophe is always used except when referring to its website, Barrons.com. The formal name, Barron's National Business and Financial Weekly, is not needed on any reference.

basic earnings per share vs. diluted earnings per share A publicly traded company will report both numbers. Basic earnings per share is net income divided by the total number of shares in the company outstanding. Diluted earnings per share includes the number of shares outstanding plus the shares that would be held by investors if all its **stock options, war-**rants and convertible securities were exercised. For companies that have issued a lot of stock options to executives, the diluted earnings-per-share number is usually lower than the basic earnings per share number.

Business news organizations differ on which number to use when writing earnings stories. Some use the basic earnings per share number, while others use the diluted earnings per share number. Check with your editor to determine which number to use. However, *EPS* is unacceptable on any reference. **($$$)**

basis point One 100th of 1 percent. Written another way, 100 basis points equal 1 percentage point. Companies and analysts will talk about a change in ratios such as profit margins or net operating margin in terms of basis points. **($$$)**

BASF SE Capitalize the name of the German-based company, the largest chemical producer in the world.

basket of goods A set of goods and services whose prices are compiled on a regular basis to track inflation. In the United States, a basket of goods tracks the consumer price index. **($$)**

bean counter A slang term for a person in a company's finance or accounting department who tracks, or is concerned with, the company's spending. Use only in direct quotes and columns.

bear market A period in which the broader stock markets fall. A bear market is considered by many to be at least a 20 percent decline in an index. Avoid using this term if the market has fallen by a smaller percentage. **($$)**

beating the gun A term that describes when an investor buys or sells a stock before the price has reacted to breaking news, such as a company issuing a warning that its earnings won't be as high as analyst expectations. **($$)**

beige book A report from the Federal Reserve that examines the economy around the country. It is released eight times a year — about two weeks before each Federal Open Market Committee meeting — and includes information gathered by each of the 12 Federal Reserve Banks about economic conditions in their regions. The release of the beige book typically results in a story by major business wire services and other business media outlets. The markets typically focus on the summary. **($$)**

Belk Inc. The Charlotte-based department store chain has stores called Belk Hudson and Hudson Belk.

beneficial owner The individual, or group of individuals, who owns a specific security. For example, shares of stock may be held by a 94-year-old woman from Thomasville, Ga., in a brokerage account. That woman is the *beneficial owner* even though the stock is under the brokerage account's name. **($$$)**

Bernanke, Ben The chairman of the Federal Reserve Board. Acceptable to use *Fed chair* or *Fed chairman* on second reference.

beta A number that measures the volatility of a stock compared with the overall market, with a 1 rating being the average for the market. A beta above 1 means the stock is more volatile than the overall market. Utility stocks, for example, typically have betas below 1, but technology stocks typically have betas above 1. A company's stock with a beta of 1.5 can be described as a stock that is 50 percent more volatile than the overall market. **($$$$)**

Better Business Bureau A nonprofit organization that sets and upholds high standards for fair and honest business behavior. The Better Business Bureau has 124 local organizations across the United States and Canada that evaluate and monitor businesses and charities. *The bureau* is acceptable on second reference.

bid The price at which an investor is willing to purchase a stock. A bid will also include the amount of shares the investor is willing to buy. **($$)**

Big Board A nickname for the New York Stock Exchange. Use only after referring to the exchange by its full name.

Big Blue Acceptable after first reference for IBM.

big-box retailer Another term for a retailer with large stores, typically more than 50,000 square feet in size. Examples include Wal-Mart, Target, Home Depot and Best Buy.

Big Pharma A term used to describe the large companies in the pharmaceutical industry. There are 33 companies in the industry with more than $3 billion in annual revenue and more than $500 million in annual **research and development** costs.

Big Three The term can no longer be used to refer to General Motors Co., Ford Motor Co. and Chrysler Group LLC as they no longer are the three biggest auto makers.

Birds Eye Foods Inc. No apostrophe in the name of the Rochester, N.Y.-based frozen food company.

BlackBerry A trademarked product from Research in Motion Ltd. Both B's are capitalized. The generic term is smartphone.

black-box accounting A term used to describe financial statements that are so complex that they are difficult to understand. Avoid using unless you can explain the accounting method being used.

Black Friday A phrase commonly used to refer to the Christmas shopping done on the Friday after Thanksgiving because it is the day that many retailers supposedly go "into the black," i.e., become profitable. It is not, however, the largest shopping day of the year in terms of the dollar value of products sold. That typically occurs on the Saturday before Christmas, according to the International Council of Shopping Centers. In eight of 10 years between 1996 and 2005, the Saturday before Christmas was the biggest shopping day in the United States. The council hasn't released data on the top shopping days since 2005. Also, Black Friday has a secondary meaning — the stock market crash in September 1869. **($$$$)**

Black Monday A phrase commonly used to refer to the stock market drops that occurred in October 1929 and October 1987. The October 1929 drop led to the Great Depression, while the October 1987 drop was the largest one-day percentage decline in stock market history. **($)**

blackout period A time period in which a contract cannot be changed, such as a retirement plan or health benefits coverage. **($$$)**

blind pool A limited partnership or stock offering with no stated goal for the funds received from the investors.

block trade A trade of at least 10,000 shares of a stock or $200,000 worth of a bond. **($$)**

Bloomberg Businessweek The business magazine is two words. The magazine was founded in 1929. After being owned by McGraw-Hill for 80 years, it was sold in 2009 to Bloomberg L.P.

Bloomberg L.P. The New York-based parent company of Bloomberg News, a financial wire service that is delivered via its terminals and to media customers. When founded in 1990, the wire service was originally called Bloomberg Business News. It now also owns radio, television, magazine and book publishing operations. When writing about the wire service and the company together, or when mentioning its founder, Michael Bloomberg, make sure to distinguish which one is being referenced.

blue chip A term used to describe a large, financially secure company. Blue-chip stocks are considered to be high quality. **($$)**

Blue Cross and Blue Shield Many different health insurers have the rights to use the name from the Blue Cross Blue Shield Association. Identify which one on first reference: *Blue Cross and Blue Shield of Alabama.*

board of directors A group of people who represent the interest of shareholders and make major policy decisions for a company. The **CEO** of a company reports to the board of directors, although this person may also be the chairman of the board.

Board members are elected at a company's annual meeting. Always lowercase.

There are *inside directors* and *outside directors*. Inside directors are those who are employees of the company. Outside directors are those who are not employed by the company, although they may be executives of other companies that do business with the company on whose board they sit.

boardroom A room where the **board of directors** of a company usually meets. Business reporters sometimes state that a decision was made "in the boardroom" when it actually wasn't. Be cautious when using this phrase. It should only be used to mean a decision by the board of directors.

Boeing Co. Now based in Chicago, not Seattle. Avoid capitalizing "the" before the name.

boiler room A term used to describe a brokerage that uses aggressive marketing tactics in an attempt to sell stocks or bonds. In some cases, the investments may be highly speculative or even fraudulent. **($$$)**

boilerplate Standardized language or common disclosures in a company's **Securities and Exchange Commission** documents, contracts or regulatory filings.

bond An investment where a company or a government entity borrows money from investors for a certain amount of time. A bond offers a rate of return for the investor, and therefore is considered safer than stocks. Bonds are also called **fixed-income securities** or **debt**. When writing about bonds issued by companies, do not state that bondholders have an ownership stake similar to shareholders. Bonds do not convey ownership unless they are **convertible bonds**. **($$)**

The Bond Buyer A newspaper published five days a week founded in 1891 that covers the municipal bond industry.

bond fund A mutual fund that invests primarily in corporate or government bonds. **($$)**

bondholder An investor who owns bonds. One word.

bond rating A grade given to a bond that indicates the financial security of the issuer. The highest rating is AAA. Anything below BBB, or Ba3 for Moody's, is considered a **junk bond**. Bonds rating D are in default for nonpayment.

bonus Additional compensation received by an employee of a company above his or her salary and other payments. A bonus is sometimes higher than the person's salary.

book building Describes the process in which an underwriter determines the price of an initial public offering. When an underwriter takes orders from clients as to how many shares they want of the **IPO** and at what price, the underwriter is said to be *building a book* for the offer. Those orders help the underwriter set the overall price for the offering. **($$$$)**

book runner The managing underwriter who maintains the books of securities sold for a new issue. Also commonly called the **lead underwriter**. **($$$$)**

book value Another term for **shareholder's equity**. It equals the value of a company's assets minus liabilities. It is the dollar amount that investors in the company would receive if the company's assets were sold for their accounting value, which may not equal their fair market value, and its liabilities were paid off.

Books-A-Million Inc. Hyphenate the name of the Birmingham, Ala.-based book retailer.

Books on Tape A trademarked product. The T is capitalized. The generic term is audio books.

bottom fisher An investor who likes to purchase stocks that have fallen dramatically in price. A bottom fisher believes the stock price will rebound. **($$)**

boutique A small firm that specializes in offering services to a few clients. A boutique investment bank may cater to a specific industry.

boycott In business, a term used to describe when consumers organize to stop using or purchasing a good or service because they disagree with a decision made by the manufacturer.

brand jacking Occurs when a third party takes a company's name and slogan and uses it for its own purposes without the company's permission. (**$$$**)

brand names Products or services that have distinguished themselves from competitors by quality, style, innovation or heavy advertising. Guard against using brand names to describe a product. For example, write *photo copies* rather than *Xeroxes*.

breakup fee A settlement negotiated as part of a merger or acquisition that would be paid by the buyer or seller if that party terminates the deal. Breakup fees are often set at a high amount to discourage other bidders. There is no hyphen, per the AP stylebook. (**$$$**)

BRIC An acronym that refers to Brazil, Russia, India and China. *BRIC* is acceptable on all references, but make sure that the countries are listed somewhere in the story. (**$$**)

broker A person who charges a commission to execute a transaction. The term can also be used to describe a firm. See **dealer**.

brokerage account Similar to a bank account, a brokerage account is where an investor places money with a broker and that money is used to execute the investor's trades.

brokerage A company that employs stock brokers to execute trades for investors.

bubble A rapid and unrealistic rise in the price of an asset. When the bubble bursts, prices collapse.

Bubble Wrap A trademarked product name. Note that it is two words. The general term is packaging bubbles.

bucket shop A brokerage firm that uses aggressive tactics to persuade investors to buy or sell stocks and bonds. The term is derogatory and should be used sparingly. Also known as a **boiler room** operation. (**$$**)

build-out An estimate of the amount of money and land needed for a development. (**$$**)

bulge bracket A term used to describe the underwriting banks that sell the bulk of the stock in an initial public offering. These are the underwriters typically listed on the **tombstone** advertisement. (**$$**)

bull market A time when investments are rising. The terms *bull market a*nd *bear market* come from how the animals attack their prey. A bull thrusts its horns up, while a bear swipes its paws down. *Bull market* should be used sparingly and never for a one- or two-day increase. **($)**

Bureau of Economic Analysis A division of the U.S. Commerce Department that tracks the country's gross domestic product, as well as the GDP for states and specific metropolitan areas. It also tracks foreign trade. Avoid BEA on all references.

Bureau of Labor Statistics A division of the U.S. Department of Labor that tracks economic data such as unemployment, inflation, the producer price index and productivity. *BLS* is acceptable on second reference.

burn rate A term used to describe how much money a company is consuming each month. *Burn rate* indicates how long it will be before the new business runs out of money. For example, a company with $15 million in funding with a burn rate of $1 million can only last for 15 months without finding additional funding or generating cash. **($$$$)**

business editor Capitalize when used as a formal title before a person's name.

business-to-business Describes transactions where one business is selling to another, such as a manufacturer selling to a wholesaler. Avoid the B2B abbreviation.

bushel A dry measure used in commodities trading, especially for grains, such as wheat.

buy (n. or v.) A rating given to a company's stock by a sell-side analyst. *Buy* or *strong buy* are typically the highest ratings an analyst gives.

buyback (n.), buy back (v.) The repurchasing of shares by a company to decrease its number of shares outstanding. A company will *buy back* those shares. A company's announcement of a buyback plan doesn't mean necessarily that the shares will actually be repurchased. Some companies will announce a buyback plan to support its stock price, but not actually repurchase the shares Also, some companies will buy back their stock to inflate their **earnings per share** numbers. The term *share repurchase* is also acceptable. **($$)**

buyout (adj., n.), buy out (v.) Another term for an **acquisition**, or when a company buys out the contract of one of its executives so that he or she will leave. A buyout of a company occurs when one company buys a controlling interest of the stock in another company.

buy-side analyst An **analyst** who works for a money manager or investment firm whose research is used solely for in-house purposes. A buy-side analyst typically makes recommendations for stocks to buy and sell for the firm's internal funds it manages for investors. See **sell-side analyst**. **($$)**

buy the dips A phrase used to describe when investors purchase shares or bonds after a decline in their price. **($$$)**

CA Inc. The Islandia, N.Y., company formerly known as Computer Associates should now be referred to as CA Inc. on first reference and CA on subsequent references.

cafeteria plan An employee benefit plan that allows workers to choose from a menu of options. The options will typically include items such as health insurance, disability insurance, life insurance, tax credits and retirement plans. **($$$)**

calendar year From Jan. 1 to Dec. 31. While many companies report their financial performance based on the calendar year, others will report using the **fiscal year.** These terms are often interchangeable unless a company's fiscal year is not the same as the calendar year.

call options An agreement that gives an investor the right but not the obligation to purchase a stock, bond or commodity at a specific price by a specific time. Owning a call option, however, does not mean that the investor actually owns the investment. See **put options. ($$$$)**

capital A vague term often used to describe the assets of a company. Capital can be cash, or a "capital asset" such as machinery, equipment or anything else of value.

capital expenditure The amount of money that a company spends each year to expand or maintain its operations. Many industries have large capital expenditure budgets each year, while others have small capital expenditure spending. Do not use the slang capex, often used by company CFOs and treasurers. **($$$)**

capital gain An increase in the value of a business asset or investment from its purchase price. However, the gain is not realized until the asset is sold. The opposite is **capital loss. ($$$$)**

capital gain distribution A payment made by a mutual fund to investors based on the realized capital gains of its investment portfolio. **($$$$)**

capital loss A loss when an investment decreases in value below its cost. The loss isn't actually recognized until the investment is sold. It's the opposite of **capital gain.**

CarMax Inc. Capitalize the M in the name of the auto retailer based in Richmond, Va.

carrying value The value of an asset on a company's balance sheet. The carrying value of an asset is often lower than its actual value if it was sold. **($$)**

cartel A group of producers of a service or a product that join together to control the supply in an effort to manipulate prices. **($$)**

cash The amount of money a company has on its books at the end of a reporting period. It is not to be confused with cash flow.

cash basis accounting An accounting method that recognizes revenue or expenses at the time cash is paid out or received. It is simpler than the **accrual accounting** method. **($$$$)**

cash cow A business line, product or asset that consistently produces money for its owners. This is a slang term. Use it sparingly, and carefully.

cash earnings Also known as pro-forma earnings. Do not use this term because it excludes items such as charges. State what items aren't included.

cash flow The amount of cash a company generates. It is calculated by adding noncash charges, such as depreciation, to the net income after taxes. Cash flow can be used as an indicator of a company's financial strength. A company can be described as having a *positive cash flow* or a *negative cash flow*. **($$)**

cash market A term used to describe the market where you can actually purchase a commodity rather than a futures contract for that commodity. **($$)**

cash reserves Cash deposits, short-term bank deposits, money market deposits and short-term securities, all of which can be converted quickly to cash. **($$)**

casualty insurance Insurance against loss of property, damage or other liabilities. A type of casualty insurance is workers' compensation insurance.

category killer A term used to describe a product, brand or service that dominates the market category. The term comes from the belief that other competitors will exit the market, leaving the category to the dominant entry.

Cemex S.A.B. de C.V. Capitalize only the first letter in the name of the building materials company based in Mexico with large operations in the United States. *Cemex* is acceptable in most first references.

cents Always spell out and lowercase when writing about earnings below $1 per share. Write *31 cents per share,* not *$.31 per share.*

certificate of deposit A savings certificate that pays interest during its term, which can be anywhere from several months to several years. *CD* is acceptable on second reference.

certificate of need A regulatory process in many states that requires a health care facility such as a hospital or nursing to apply for and receive approval to expand its services or to convert beds to other services. Avoid CON on all references. **($$$)**

certified public accountant A designation given by the American Institute of Certified Public Accountants for someone who has passed its exam and meets certain work requirements. *CPA* is acceptable on second reference.

chairman of the board The most senior executive, in terms of position, in an organization. The chair is responsible for running the annual meeting and the meetings of the board of directors. He or she may be a figurehead, appointed for prestige, and may have no role in the day-to-day running of the organization. Sometimes the roles of chair and chief executive officer are combined. *Chairwoman* is acceptable if the person is female. Capitalize before a name.

channel stuffing A term used to describe when a company induces suppliers and retailers to purchase more of its product near the end of a period to make its financial results look better. Channel stuffing can backfire on a company by reducing future sales and profits. **($$$$)**

Chap Stick A trademarked product. Note that it is two words. The generic term is lip balm.

Chapter 7 A bankruptcy court filing by a company in which the business plans to liquidate its assets and close operations. Sometimes, a Chapter 11 filing can be converted into a Chapter 7 by the court if a business can't come to a reorganization agreement with its creditors.

Chapter 11 A bankruptcy court filing by a company or an individual where the debtor proposes paying off some, but not all, of its debt. The filing essentially asks the court to forgive some of the money owed.

Chapter 13 A bankruptcy court filing by an individual who proposes to repay all of his or her debt during an extended period of time.

charge A one-time expense by a company that negatively affects earnings. **($$)**

Charles Schwab Corp. Avoid capitalizing "the" before the company name.

chartered financial analyst A designation given by the CFA Institute to a **financial analyst** that measures his or her competency and integrity. *CFA* is acceptable on second reference.

Cheesecake Factory Inc. Avoid capitalizing "the" before the company name of this Calabasas Hills, Calif.-based company.

cherry picking Selecting a sample to show what you want to show rather than to show what's really happening. For example, a mutual fund may show in an advertisement its one-year performance because it beats the overall market rather than its 10-year performance, which underperforms the market. **($$)**

Chicago Board of Trade The world's oldest futures and commodities exchange. It merged with the Chicago Mercantile Exchange in 2007. Do not use CBOT on any reference.

Chicago Mercantile Exchange A 1919 spinoff from the Chicago Board of Trade, the Chicago Mercantile Exchange trades financial and commodity derivatives. It merged with the Chicago Board of Trade in 2007 and the New York Mercantile Exchange in 2008. The terms *Chicago Merc* and *Merc* are acceptable on second reference. Do not use CME on any reference.

Chick-fil-A Inc. Note the hyphens and capitalization of the privately held restaurant chain based in Atlanta.

chief executive officer The top management position at any company. The chief executive officer of a company typically sets the strategic direction of the business. *CEO* is acceptable on first reference.

chief financial officer The person at a company who oversees its financial statements and is also responsible for the financing, such as stock and bond offerings. The *CFO* is also typically the main point person at a company who deals with investors and analysts. *CFO* is acceptable on second reference.

chief information officer A title often used for the person at a company in charge of information technology. This person typically reports to the **chief operating officer** or **president** of a company and has grown in importance in recent years. *CIO* is acceptable on second reference.

chief operating officer The officer responsible for the day-to-day management of a company who usually reports to the **chief executive officer**. *COO* is acceptable on second reference.

chief risk officer An executive responsible for ensuring that a company is in compliance with regulations and has minimized potential damage to its reputation, financial results and operations. Do not use CRO on any reference. **($$$)**

Chinese wall A term used to describe the supposed separation between the investment banking and research operations of a brokerage house. Many firms were criticized for having little to no separation between the two areas in the 1990s and early part of the 21st century.

churning Unnecessary trading in accounts, solely to increase brokers' commissions. It's unethical. **($$)**

CiCi's Enterprises LP Both Cs are capitalized in the name of the Coppell, Texas-based restaurant operator.

Cigna Corp. A health insurance and benefits company based in Philadelphia. Although the company spells its name with all capital letters, in stories it should be written as Cigna. The letters came from a combination of Connecticut General Corp. and INA Corp., which stood for Insurance Company of North America.

Citgo Petroleum Corp. Lowercase the first name of the Houston-based gas retailer after the C.

class action A lawsuit filed by one or more people on behalf of many other people who may be in a similar situation. Class-action lawsuits may be difficult and are expensive, but they allow people who can't afford to file a lawsuit individually to band together.

classes of shares Types of shares in a company that have different voting rights. For example, some companies may have Class A shares and Class B shares where Class A shares may have 10 votes each while Class B shares have only 1 vote each. Many companies set up the different classes when they go public to allow families to maintain control of the company. Note that Class is always capitalized.

clearing house A third party that settles trades for futures and options

contracts. Members of a commodity exchange, for example, are required to clear their trades through a clearing house. **($$$)**

Clif Bar & Co. The Berkeley, Calif.-based natural foods company has just one f in its name.

closed-end fund A publicly traded investment company that raises money in an initial public offering and has a fixed number of shares. Such funds trade like stocks and have little in common with mutual funds, which are also known as open-end funds. **($$)**

closed shop A business where union membership is a condition for employment.

closely held When there are a few shareholders controlling a company. It may still be publicly traded. **($$)**

closing bell A term used to describe the close of the markets. In the United States, that time is 4 p.m. EST. It's also the name of a CNBC show.

CNA Financial Corp. Because each letter is pronounced, capitalize CNA in all references to the Chicago-based insurer.

CNBC A business news cable television network. As part of the National Broadcasting Co., it is a subsidiary of General Electric and is based in Englewood Cliffs, N.J. The network went on the air in April 1989 and is now considered the primary business news venue on television. A competitor, Fox Business Network, started in October 2007. CNBC stands for Consumer News & Business Channel, but *CNBC* should be used on all references. CNBC is responsible for launching the careers of many business journalists, including Maria Bartiromo.

CNET.com An online technology news service. It was acquired by CBS Corp. in 2008.

coattail investing A term used to describe when investors mimic the investment strategy of well-known investors, such as Warren Buffett. **($$)**

Coke A trademarked product. Can also be referred to as Coca-Cola. The company, which is called Coca-Cola Co., recently dropped the word Classic from the end of the product.

cold calling Making unsolicited phone calls in an attempt to drum up new business. Be careful using this term, as it sometimes has a negative connotation. **($$$)**

collar A strategy that limits both the upside and the downside of an investment. A collar is also used in some acquisitions where stock is used as currency. **($$$$)**

collateralized debt obligation An investment security backed by a pool of bonds or loans. Do not use CDO on second reference. Do not hyphenate. **($$$$$)**

collateralized mortgage obligation An investment security backed by mortgages that has different levels of when investors are repaid. Do not use CMO on second reference. Use *pool* or *investment*. Do not hyphenate. **($$$$$)**

combined ratio A measure of profitability for a property and casualty insurance company. The combined ratio is the value of the claims paid plus the company's expenses divided by the dollar value of the premium collected. A combined ratio below 100 percent means that the company is making a profit from its insurance operations. An insurance company with a combined ratio of 105 percent is paying out $1.05 in claims and expenses for every $1 it collects in premiums. It may still be profitable, however, because of profits from investments. **($$)**

commas A common problem in business reporting. The tendency is to use commas in the wrong places. For example, there is no comma before a company's name and Co., Inc. or Corp. It should be written as *Home Depot Inc.* not *Home Depot, Inc.,* even if the company places the comma there. Commas should also be used in numbers of 1,000 and above, including monetary amounts. Write *The chief executive's salary rose to $450,000, up $50,000 from his salary in 2008.*

commercial paper Unsecured, short-term debt issued by a company. Such debt is typically used to finance **accounts receivable** and inventory at a company, and it is not registered with the Securities and Exchange Commission, like other debt issued by a company, because it is scheduled to be paid back in less than nine months. **($$$$)**

commission A fee charged by a broker or an investment adviser, typically for services such as buying or selling stock for the customer.

committee names Always lower case and never abbreviate. For example, *The executive compensation committee of the board decided to raise salaries in 2009.*

commodity A good that is bought and sold by investors. Types of commodities include wheat, corn, beef, gold, silver and platinum. The term has recently also been used to refer to technology products that have become common.

Commodity Futures Trading Commission A federal regulatory agency formed in 1974 that regulates the commodities and futures markets, much in the same way that the Securities and Exchange Commission regulates the stock market. Do not use CFTC on second reference. Use commission instead.

common stock The most common type of publicly traded shares. The common stock holders are the ones that vote on the board of directors and shareholder proposals. See **preferred stock**.

company Always abbreviate as Co. when used at the end of the company's name on first reference. Do not use at the end of the company's name on second reference. Spell out and lower case when it stands alone.

company names The full company name should be used only on first reference, including Co., Inc., Corp. and Ltd. For example, *Hewlett-Packard Co.* on first reference, but *Hewlett-Packard* on second reference. Do not use all capital letters unless they are individually pronounced, such as *BMW*. Do not use symbols or exclamation points. Use an ampersand only if it is part of the company name. Do not capitalized *the* even if it is capitalized by the company. Company names in this stylebook are primarily listed because of capitalization and punctuation issues.

company nicknames IBM is often referred to as Big Blue after the first reference. However, please avoid using nicknames unless they will be familiar to the average reader. For example, the term *Big Red* might be acceptable to business news readers in Atlanta for a story about Coca-Cola

Co., but note that there's a carbonated soft drink company, based in Waco, Texas, named Big Red Ltd.

Conference Board A nonprofit organization that makes economics-based forecasts and assesses trends in the marketplace that are useful to business reporters.

conference call An event in which investors call a special phone number and hear the management of their company comment on the financial results of a recently completed quarter or another important event. Business journalists can listen to conference calls, but few companies allow them to ask questions.

conglomerate A company that owns businesses in many different industries, including industries that may not be related. For example, General Electric Co. owns businesses that make airplane engines and dishwashers as well as the NBC television network. **($)**

consensus analyst estimate The average earnings estimate for a company based on the predictions of all of the analysts covering the company. The estimate could be for an upcoming quarter or for a year. Business reporters often compare the consensus estimate with the actual results when writing earnings stories. **($$)**

consolidated financial statement A term used to describe the financial statements of a company and its subsidiaries. **($$)**

consumer spending The purchase of goods and services by consumers, also known as consumption and personal consumption expenditures. Consumer spending totals two-thirds of the U.S. gross domestic product.

construction spending Data that represent the payout by builders on residential and nonresidential structures. It is compiled monthly by the Census Bureau and is split between private and public construction.

Consumer Confidence Index A measurement by the Conference Board on whether consumers are feeling optimistic or pessimistic about the economy. The University of Michigan has a similar measurement called the **Index of Consumer Sentiment.** The Conference Board survey focuses on labor conditions, while the Michigan survey focuses on financial conditions. Use *index* for both on second reference.

consumer credit Debt used by consumers to purchase a good or service. Examples are credit card debt and auto loans. Consumer credit is also referred to as *consumer debt.* **($$)**

consumer price index A monthly measure of the price change of consumer goods such as gasoline, food and automobiles. It is compiled by the **Bureau of Labor Statistics** and released monthly. The story focuses on the change in the index for urban workers, or CPI-U, which covers about 87 percent of the population. *CPI* is acceptable on second reference. (**$$**)

Consumer Product Safety Commission The federal agency that protects consumers against faulty products. Its jurisdiction covers product safety for more than 15,000 products, and it can force a recall of a product. *CPSC* is acceptable on second reference.

continuing claims A number compiled by the Department of Labor that measures the sum of all unemployed workers receiving benefits in a given week. (**$$**)

contrarian An investment strategy in which assets are purchased when most investors are selling and sold when most investors are buying. (**$$**)

conversion The process in which a company changes its ownership structure, typically from one where the business is owned by its customers, such as a mutual insurance company, to one where the business is owned by stockholders. (**$$$**)

convertible bond A bond that can be converted to stock in the company,

usually at the discretion of the investor. *Convertible* is acceptable on second reference. (**$$$$**)

cook the books A term used to describe when a company uses fraudulent accounting. Do not use this term unless charges have been filed against the company or its auditor.

core competency A term used to describe the main strength of a company. (**$$**)

core earnings The profit derived from a company's main business. For example, the core earnings of an auto company would include the profits it makes from making cars and trucks, but it would exclude profits or losses from a nonvehicle business such as the savings and loan that Ford once owned. (**$$**)

Corporate Library LLC An independent research firm based in Portland, Maine, that acts as a watchdog on behalf of shareholders.

corporation The most common form of business organization. The organization is ongoing, and the owners' liability is limited. Abbreviate as *Corp.* when used on first reference as part of a company's formal name. Do not use on the second reference of a company.

correction A Wall Street euphemism for falling securities prices. Do not use this term as prices aren't mistakes. (**$$**)

cost of capital The necessary profit needed for a company project, such as the building of a new warehouse. **($$)**

cost of goods sold The cost required to make a product. It includes the cost of both the ingredients or parts and the labor. Do not abbreviate as COGS. Use *cost* on second reference. **($$)**

cost of living The amount of money needed to purchase housing and necessary goods. A *cost of living adjustment* increases or decreases someone's income to reflect changes caused by inflation or a contraction. Do not abbreviate as COL or COLA on second reference. **($)**

counteroffer A response to an acquisition offer when the company in play wants better terms before being acquired. Can also use *counter* as the verb.

counterparty The other party in a financial transaction.

coupon The interest rate on a bond when it's issued. **($$)**

courtesy titles The New York Times business desk and The Wall Street Journal still use them, such as Mr., Ms. and Mrs., but virtually no other business media outlet does. Avoid unless you're writing for one of these.

coverage initiated When a sell-side analyst begins coverage of a company's stock. *Merrill Lynch & Co. analyst Barney Google initiated coverage on Coca-Cola Co. on Thursday with a "buy" rating and a $50 price target.*

Cramer, Jim The co-founder of TheStreet.com who also has a regular show on CNBC called "Mad Money." Cramer, a former professional investor, has been criticized for giving bad investment advice through the media. A jump in the stock price of a company mentioned on Cramer's show is known as the *Cramer effect.*

Crayola A trademarked product. The generic word is crayons.

crash A major, sudden decline in a market. The term *crash* is not used unless the market has fallen by at least 20 percent. **($$)**

credit When a borrower receives something of value now and agrees to repay the lender at a future date. The term can also refer to the borrowing capacity a person or company might have.

credit crunch A time period when it becomes more difficult and costly for consumers or companies to borrow money. It usually follows a period in which consumers default on loans in higher-than-normal amounts, causing lenders to adjust their borrowing requirements. *Credit crisis* is not acceptable. A **credit crisis** means there's almost no borrowed money to be had.

credit default swap A contract used to hedge or speculate on a company's ability to repay its debt. The contract pays the buyer should the company default. **($$$$)**

credit spread The difference between the yields of a Treasury and company debt that have the same rating and the same maturity. The spread reflects the additional yield that an investor can earn by investing in a security with more risk.

credit union A financial institution that competes with banks and **savings and loans** for consumer deposits and loans. Credit unions are cooperatives that are owned and controlled by members. They are regulated by the **National Credit Union Administration**.

creditor A person or company that is owed money.

Crispin Porter & Bogusky Use the ampersand, not the plus sign, in the name of the Miami-based advertising agency.

Crock-Pot A trademarked product. Note the hyphen and capital P. The generic term is electric earthenware cooker.

curb trading Trading that occurs through computers or on the telephone after the market has closed. Also known as **after-hours trading**.

currency A generally accepted form of money, usually referring to paper money but can also include coins. The currency market is the largest in the world in terms of the amount traded each day.

CUSIP number An identification number given to all stocks and bonds. Stands for Committee on Uniform Securities Identification Procedures. Capitalize CUSIP in all references. **($$)**

CVS Caremark Corp. Use the full name when referring to the company. Use just *CVS* when referring to the drug store operations or a specific store.

Cyber Monday A term used to describe the Internet-based Christmas shopping that occurs on the Monday after Thanksgiving. However, it is typically not the biggest Internet shopping day of the year. The phrase was coined by the National Retail Federation as a marketing gimmick. Avoid using it.

damp (adj.), dampen (v.) Use *dampen* as the verb in instances such as, *The global recession continued to dampen sales of its products.*

Day-Glo A trademarked product. Note the hyphen and capital G. The generic name is fluorescent colors.

day trading When an investor holds positions for very short time periods, such as minutes or hours, and makes numerous trades during a day. Avoid using this term for traditional investors.

datelines A dateline indicates where the reporter did the bulk of the reporting for his or her story, no matter where the major action in the story took place. If that location has little or no bearing on the story, use no dateline. For example, a story written from the South Korean capital on the North Korean economy should use a Seoul dateline because the reporting location is significant. A story being reported from Cleveland about the Cincinnati economy, however, should carry no dateline because the reporting location has no bearing on the story. If the bulk of the reporting took place in Cincinnati, then a Cincinnati dateline is appropriate.

dead cat bounce A temporary recovery in a market after a prolonged drop, typically followed by a continued decline. **($$$$)**

deal A transaction such as a merger, acquisition or issuance of stock. Do not use on first reference.

Deal, The A New York-based business publication that focuses on covering mergers and acquisitions.

dealer A person or a firm willing to buy or sell investments for its own account. The term is not the same as **broker.** A broker is someone who buys and sells on behalf of clients.

death tax Avoid this term because opponents of estate taxes have long used it to express their opposition. Use *estate tax* instead.

debenture A type of debt that is not secured by collateral or an asset. **($$$)**

debt Money owed by a person or a company.

debt-to-capital ratio A measurement of a company's financial leverage, it is calculated by dividing a company's debt by its shareholder equity plus debt. When a company issues debt to make an acquisition, for example, it may then try to pay down that debt to lower its debt-to-capital ratio. (**$$$$**)

debt-to-equity ratio A company's total long-term debt expressed as a percentage of shareholders' equity. (**$$$$**)

debtor A person or company that owes money.

debtor-in-possession financing Money that a company in bankruptcy court receives from lenders to continue operating its business. These lenders are first in line to repaid when the company reorganizes its debt. *DIP financing* is acceptable on second reference. (**$$**)

deductible The amount of a covered loss that an insurance customer pays before the insurer starts paying. The higher the deductible, the lower the premiums paid by the customer.

deed A legal document conveying title to a piece of property.

DeepFreeze A trademarked product. The F is capitalized although it's one word. The generic word is freezer.

default When a borrower fails to make payments on its debt when it comes due.

deferred revenue Revenue collected but not yet earned by a company. An example is subscriptions. Deferred

revenue is also referred as *unearned revenue* by some companies.

deficit When liabilities exceed assets, or expenses exceed profits. The term is also common to describe when a country's imports exceed its exports.

deflation A general decline in prices. Long-term deflation can have a negative effect on the economy. (**$$**)

delisted When the shares of a company are removed from trading on a stock market because they no longer meet the market's requirements, such as an average minimum stock price. (**$$**)

Department of Justice A federal government agency that, along with the Federal Trade Commission, reviews every merger and acquisition agreement. Use *Justice Department* or *department* on second reference.

Department of Labor A federal government agency that oversees business-related issues such as workplace safety and unemployment benefits. Many states also have a labor department. The terms *Labor Department* or *department* are acceptable on second reference.

departments Companies often have departments. Lowercase them, such as *information technology department*, unless they have a formal name, such as the *O'Neill Executive Department*.

depreciation A noncash accounting charge that reduces the value of an asset. If a company purchases a machine for $1 million, it may depreciate the value over 10 years, recording a noncash expense of $100,000 for each of those years. The term can also be used to describe the change in value of a currency compared to another currency. **($$$)**

depression A severe and prolonged **recession** in the economy marked by declining economic activity, high unemployment and sometimes falling prices. **($$$$)**

deregulation When the government relaxes its regulation of an industry, typically to create more competition.

derivative An investment whose price is determined by an underlying asset. Futures contracts and swaps are types of derivatives. **($$$$)**

devaluation A downward adjustment in a country's currency exchange rate in relation to other currencies. It is always expressed as a **percent**.

DHL Acceptable on all references for the delivery company. The Bonn, Germany-based parent company's formal name is Deutsche Post DHL.

diluted earnings per share Earnings per share calculated by including the number of shares that would be outstanding if all of the stock options and warrants were exercised. For companies that have issued millions of stock options to executives, the diluted EPS number is lower than or equal to the basic EPS number. See **basic earnings per share.**

dilutive (n.) An acquisition that will decrease the acquiring company's earnings per share. As a general rule, a dilutive **merger** or **acquisition** occurs when the **price-to-earnings ratio** paid for the target firm is less than that of the acquiring firm. **($$)**

DirecTV Group Inc. Only one T in the El Segundo, Calif.-based direct broadcast satellite service.

director A member of the board of a company.

disclosure statement A document that outlines the terms of a loan, including the interest rate, fees and amount borrowed.

discount When the price of a bond is lower than the **par** value. If a **bond** with a par value of $1,000 is selling at $990, it is selling at a discount. **($$)**

discount broker A stockbroker who carries out buy and sell orders at a reduced commission rate but provides no investment advice.

discount rate The interest rate that financial institutions are charged when borrowing short term from the Federal Reserve. It can also be referred to as a *rediscount rate*. **($$$$)**

Dish Network Corp. Capitalize only the first letter in the first name of the Englewood, Colo.-based direct satellite provider.

discretionary income, disposable income These two terms are often used wrongly, or for each other. *Disposable* income is gross income minus the taxes paid on that income. *Discretionary* income is the gross income minus taxes paid and minus expenses such as housing, food and transportation needed to maintain a normal lifestyle. **($$)**

disinflation A decrease in the rate of **inflation**. Prices are not declining. Disinflation simply means that prices are not rising as fast as they were in the past. **($$$$)**

Disposall A trademarked product. The generic term is garbage disposer.

distressed sale When a company is sold to another company because it is in financial trouble and might go under without becoming part of another entity. Can also refer to the sale of stock. The acquirer typically receives the assets at a low price.

divest To sell an operation.

dividend A payment distributed to stockholders. Dividends may be in the form of cash, stock or property. All dividends are declared by the board of directors. When writing about dividends, specify the time period.

dividend reinvestment plan An option that allows investors to purchase additional shares of stock in a company by using their **dividend** payments, usually without broker's fees. Do not use DRIP on any reference. *Plan* is acceptable on second reference. **($)**

division Companies often have divisions. Lowercase unless they have a proper name, such as the Chevrolet Division of General Motors.

doctor's hospital Some local hospitals, such as the one in Augusta, Ga., that use this name have an apostrophe, while others, such as the one in Shreveport, La., don't. Check and use the local preference.

dog-and-pony show When investment banks and executives of a company selling securities visit potential investors in an attempt to persuade them to invest in the offering. The term **road show** is preferred, as dog-and-pony show is considered pejorative.

Dolan Co. A company based in Minneapolis that is the parent of weekly business newspapers, including the Long Island Business News, Mississippi Business Journal, Colorado Springs Business Journal, Idaho Business Review and the Daily Journal of Commerce in Portland, Ore. Its primary business, however, is in providing business data to lawyers and other professionals.

dollar The official name of the currency in many countries, including the United States, Canada, Australia, New Zealand and Singapore.

dollar-cost averaging An investment technique where the investor purchases a specific dollar amount of a security at regular intervals, regardless of the price. Do not use DCA on any reference. **($$$$)**

dot-com A term used to describe the technology industry, particularly companies that operate primarily on the Internet. The hyphen is per AP style.

Dow Jones Industrial Average A popular indicator that tracks the price average of 30 stocks. Operated by The Wall Street Journal and Dow Jones & Co., the index started in May 1896 with 12 stocks. In 2009, the average replaced General Motors Corp. and Citigroup Inc. with Travelers Cos. and Cisco Systems Inc. The stock that has been in the index the longest is General Electric Co., which has been there since 1907. On second reference, use *average* or *Dow*. *DJIA* is not acceptable on any reference.

Dow Jones & Co. The parent company of The Wall Street Journal, Marketwatch.com, Dow Jones Newswires and Barron's. It is currently owned by News Corp. The ampersand is used on first reference. *Dow Jones* is acceptable on second reference.

Dow Jones Newswires The newswire subsidiary of Dow Jones & Co. It competes with Bloomberg, Reuters and the Associated Press. The full name should be used on all references to distinguish it from the parent company.

downgrade (v.) A term used to describe when an analyst lowers his or her rating on a stock. To downgrade a stock would mean to lower a rating from "strong buy" to "buy" or from "buy" to "hold," for example. Do not use as a noun.

downsize A euphemistic term often used by companies to describe layoffs or the elimination of specific jobs or lines of business. It should be avoided in all cases, except in quotes. Also known as rightsizing.

downturn (n.) A negative change.

Dr Pepper Snapple Group Inc. As with the soft drink, there is no period in the Plano, Texas-based company's name.

Droid A **smartphone** designed by Motorola that uses Google's Android software. It should be lowercase after the D in all references.

due diligence An investigation of a potential investment or acquisition. In some cases, performing due diligence is a legal obligation.

dumping An action in international trade where a manufacturer in one country sends a large amount of a good into another country at a price below the manufacturer's domestic price. **($$$)**

Dumpster A trademarked brand. The generic term is trash bin.

Dunkin' Donuts The Canton, Mass.-based parent company is Dunkin' Brands Inc., which also owns the Baskin-Robbins brand. It spells doughnuts differently from Krispy Kreme Doughnuts Inc.

E.I. du Pont de Nemours & Co. The formal name of the Wilmington, Del.-based chemical company. *DuPont* is acceptable on second reference.

durable goods Products with a life span of more than three years, such as refrigerators, televisions, microwaves, automobiles and furniture. The opposite is **soft goods.**

durable goods orders An economic indicator compiled by the Census Bureau that tracks new orders with manufacturers for goods in the near term. In addition to durable goods orders, the government also measures shipments and inventory. The data is released about the fourth week of the following month, and the story focus is on total orders, nontransportation orders, nondefense orders and inventories. **($$)**

Dutch auction A public offering in which the price of the offering is set after taking in bids and determining the highest price at which the entire offering can be sold back to a company. For example, let's say that 200 shares are to be sold. If one investor offers to buy 100 shares at $20, but another investor offers to sell 100 shares at $18, then all of the shares will be sold at $20. The name comes from the traditional form of auction in the Netherlands, where products are sold simultaneously to equal high bidders. **($$$$$)**

early withdrawal The removal of money from an investment, or a retirement account, before its term has expired. Early withdrawal typically results in the person paying a penalty. **($$)**

earnings guidance A term used to describe when a company provides analysts and investors with a range of expected earnings. For example, a company could issue a press release saying it expects its first-quarter earnings to be between 18 cents per share and 22 cents per share. That would be earnings guidance. **($$)**

earnings momentum When a company's earnings per share is increasing or decreasing from previous quarters. Positive earnings momentum typically occurs when a company's revenue is rising or when it has cut its costs. For earnings to have momentum, the trend needs to occur for at least three consecutive quarters. **($$)**

earnings per share A company's profits divided by the number of outstanding shares. Company earnings are typically reported by business journalists in terms of net income first, and then earnings per share. Do not use EPS on any reference. See **basic earnings per share** and **diluted earnings per share.**

earnings story guidelines Nearly every business journalist at some time will write a story about a public company's earnings. Some will even write a story about a private company's results. The following guidelines are important to consider in such stories:

- When calculating the earnings growth or decline, focus on the net income or net loss, not the earnings per share. Companies can manipulate their earnings per share growth by decreasing the number of shares outstanding through share repurchase programs.

- Leads need to emphasize why a company's earnings rose or fell during the quarter. Don't just tell the reader that the earnings rose or fell by a certain percentage. They'll want to know the reason.

- Context, context, context. If a company's earnings have fallen after quarters of increases, then you'll need to tell the reader the last quarter in which earnings fell. Was there a loss in the quarter? Then tell the reader when the last quarterly loss occurred. Net income rose 49 percent? When was the last quarter that profits rose faster?

- Listen to the conference call. Sometimes, the story is not the press release with the numbers, but what the executives say to the analysts and investors later in the day. One telltale sign is to watch how the stock price reacts while you're listening to the call. If the price begins to move up or down dramatically, then something newsworthy was said.
- Compare a company's quarterly earnings with the same quarter from the previous year, not the previous quarter. Many businesses are cyclical, making the better comparison the same time a year ago. You can't compare, for example, Coke's second-quarter earnings with the first quarter because it's hotter in the second quarter and more people are thirsty.
- When writing about earnings, focus on the most-recent earnings first before mentioning the same quarter a year earlier. For example, write *Earnings rose 25 percent to $4.5 billion from $3.6 billion in the same time period a year ago,* not *Earnings rose 25 percent from $3.6 billion in the time period a year ago to $4.5 billion.*
- Whom are you going to quote? Increasingly, investors in the stock are being quoted in stories about the earnings, not buy-side analysts. While both have a bias, the investors have less of a conflict of interest.

earnings warning When a company announces that its earnings will not meet current Wall Street projections.

eBay Inc. Lowercase the first letter in the name of the San Jose, Calif.-based online reseller unless it begins a sentence. Capitalize the B in all references.

EBIT Earnings before interest and taxes. The preferred term is **operating income.**

EBITDA A company's earnings before interest, taxes, depreciation and amortization. Because EBITDA is not specified by **generally accepted accounting principles,** or GAAP, a company can change what is included in these earnings from quarter to quarter. When writing about a company's earnings, it's OK to mention *EBITDA,* but make sure that the company's net income or loss is also reported. That's the more conservative reflection of its performance. **($$$)**

E-commerce Sales of goods and services where an order is placed by the buyer or price and terms are negotiated by the Internet. Payment may or may not be made online. E-commerce sales data is collected by the Census Bureau and released quarterly.

economic indicator Data typically collected by the federal government that tells investors or consumers which way the economy might be moving. An economic indicator could be the unemployment rate, the **consumer price index**, the **gross domestic product** or retail sales, among many examples.

Economist, The A weekly magazine based in England that covers international issues and the world economy. Founded in 1843, it has gained a wider following in the United States in the past decade. *The* is always capitalized in the magazine's name. Although it is printed on glossy paper, the publication considers itself a newspaper, a throwback to a former version.

economy The production and consumption of goods and services in a geographic area. Economies can be entire countries, states, counties or a **metropolitan statistical area.**

effective date The date at which securities can start trading, as determined by the Securities and Exchange Commission. The effective date is typically used when referring to an **initial public offering.**

efficiency ratio A ratio used to calculate a bank's efficiency. It's typically calculated by dividing noninterest expenses by revenue, although some banks calculate it differently. **($$)**

EDGAR Stands for Electronic Data Gathering, Analysis and Retrieval. It's the system used by the Securities and Exchange Commission to compile documents from publicly traded companies. *EDGAR* is acceptable in all references. **($$$)**

84 Lumber Co. The privately held retailer always uses the number 84 in its name. Its headquarters, however, is in Eighty Four, Pa.

Electronic Arts Inc. The Redwood City, Calif.-based video game manufacturer can be referred to as *EA* on second reference.

employee stock ownership plan A plan where a company allows its employees to buy shares of the business. These plans are increasing in popularity with small and private businesses. Do not use ESOP on any reference. **($$)**

Enron Corp. A former Houston-based energy company that collapsed and filed for bankruptcy in late 2001 after one of the largest financial and accounting frauds in history was uncovered. Be cautious when comparing a company to Enron.

ensure, insure To ensure means to make sure something happens. To insure means to issue an insurance policy. The words are not interchangeable.

Enterprise Rent-A-Car Co. The St. Louis-based car rental company is the only one in the industry that hyphenates rent-a-car in its name.

enterprise value A measure of a company's value. It is calculated by adding stock market capitalization, debt and preferred shares. **($$$$)**

Entrepreneur A monthly business magazine that caters to small companies.

Environmental Protection Agency The federal agency whose job is to protect the environment and human health by preventing the release of harmful items into the environment. The agency can ban the use of certain products, and it can fine companies for violating environmental laws. The use of *EPA* is acceptable on second reference.

Equal Employment Opportunity Commission The federal agency created in 1964 to investigate claims of employment discrimination on the basis of race, color, sex, age, natural origin and religion. Its jurisdiction has since been expanded to include discrimination based on disability. The abbreviation *EEOC* is acceptable on second reference.

equity A synonym for a stock or another investment that conveys ownership. *Stock* is the preferred term. In terms of real estate, it's the difference between the market value of a home or a commercial property and the amount owed on the mortgage. **($)**

equity fund A mutual fund that invests primarily in stocks. *Stock fund* is the preferred term. **($$)**

errors and omissions insurance A policy purchased by a company or an individual that protects against claims for inadequate or shoddy work. *E&O insurance* is acceptable on second reference. **($$$)**

escalator clause A part of a contract that allows one party to pass along the increasing cost to the other party. Escalator clauses typically come into play when **inflation** increases costs. **($$$$$)**

establishment survey One of the ways in which the unemployment rate is determined by the U.S. Department of Labor. The establishment survey questions 350,000 businesses with 39 million workers about the number of workers they have employed in the past month.

E-Trade Financial Corp. The New York-based online broker capitalizes all of the letters in "Trade" and a star symbol between the E and Trade. Avoid and use an en dash or hyphen and lowercase letters.

euro The official currency of the **European Union**. It was introduced in 1999, though euro banknotes and coins didn't enter use till 2002. Not all countries in Europe use the euro as their currency. Great Britain still uses the pound.

European Union A group of European countries that participate in the world economy as one. The theory behind the European Union is to create a trade zone with no barriers. There are 27 countries in the union. They are Austria, Belgium, Bulgaria, Cyprus, Czech Republic, Denmark, Estonia, Finland, France, Germany, Greece, Hungary, Ireland, Italy, Latvia, Lithuania, Luxembourg, Malta, the Netherlands, Poland, Portugal, Romania, Slovakia, Slovenia, Spain, Sweden and United Kingdom. *EU* is acceptable on second reference.

exchange A market where securities, commodities, options or futures are traded.

exchange rate The number of shares of the acquiring company that shareholders will receive for one share of the acquired company that they hold. This rate is typically reported high in an **acquisition** story. The exchange rate is also the measurement of a currency in terms of other currencies. **($$)**

exchange-traded funds An investment that trades on an exchange. The value of the fund is based on the assets it holds, such as stocks or bonds. Many exchange-traded funds track an index, such as the Standard & Poor's 500. Use *ETF* on second reference. **($$$$)**

ex-dividend The date on which stock buyers will not receive a dividend that has been declared by a company. If a company announces a dividend on Oct. 15, and says its ex-dividend date is Oct. 25, then investors who purchase the stock on Oct. 25 will not receive the dividend when it is paid. **($$$$)**

executive compensation The amount of money and other compensation that an executive receives for working at a company, including the value of items such as country club memberships and stock options. The executive's compensation can be found in the company's **proxy statement**, also known as a DEF 14A filing with the Securities and Exchange Commission. When writing about an executive's compensation, use the total compensation amount in the proxy, and compare it with the total compensation amount from the previous year.

This differs from AP Stylebook policy in writing about executive compensation. The AP guidelines for executive compensation stories state that the number in the proxy statement should not be used, and the AP has its own formula for executive compensation.

Here are some other potential newsworthy items to look for when writing about executive compensation:

- The perks given to executives, such as country club memberships and personal use of corporate jets and cars. These sometimes are worth more than the salary or bonus given to an executive.

- The compensation committee report. This often discloses how the company determined the **CEO's** pay, and whether he or she is in line for a pay increase.
- Outside shareholder proposals. In recent years, these proposals, which are voted on by all stockowners, have increasingly focused on limiting huge compensation packages.
- The stock option chart. Given the increased focus on the timing of grants, reporters should be looking at when companies gave options.
- Relationships between board members and the company. This is where you find out whether a board member's company has been doing business with the company whose board he or she sits on. Examine whether the amount of that business has increased or decreased in the past year.

existing home sales The resale of existing homes by current owners to new owners. Existing home sales are a majority of home sales in the United States. The term is not to be confused with **new-home sales**. These data are compiled by the National Association of Realtors on a monthly basis and are released in the last week of the following month. The story focuses on the level and the monthly change in total sales.

exit strategy How a major investor plans to sell its stake in a company. A hedge fund or venture capital fund that has acquired a major stake in a company may implement its exit strategy by selling the company to another company or have that company hold an **initial public offering**.

exotic instrument An option with a nonstandard feature, such as an option that allows an investor to select the exercise price. **($$)**

expectations index Part of the Consumer Confidence Index that measures how consumers think the economy will be in six months.

Expedia Inc. Write as Expedia.com when referring to the Bellevue, Wash.-based company's online travel service site.

expense ratio The cost, as a percent of assets, that investors pay for a mutual fund's expenses. **($$)**

extraordinary item Gains or losses in a company's financial statement that are unusual in nature. For example, losses resulting from a hurricane or tornado would be listed as an extraordinary item in an insurance company's financial statement. See **nonrecurring charge. ($$)**

Exxon Mobil Corp. An Irving, Texas-based company formed by a 1999 takeover. *ExxonMobil* is acceptable on second reference.

Facebook Inc. Use Facebook.com when writing about the Palo Alto, Calif.-based company's social networking site.

face value The dollar value of a security when issued. It's also called the **par value** or **par. ($$)**

fair market value The price that an asset would bring in the marketplace, assuming that the market is acting normally.

fairness opinion A professional evaluation by an investment bank or other party as to whether the terms of a merger, acquisition, spin-off or other transaction are fair. Details of a fairness opinion are often included in a Form S-4. **($$$)**

Fannie Mae The shortened name for the Federal National Mortgage Association, a government-sponsored entity created to expand the mortgage market. It purchases loans from lenders and then packages those loans into pools that are sold to investors. *Fannie Mae* is acceptable in all references.

Fannie May Confections Inc. Note the *May* spelling in the name of the Chicago-based candy company, which also owns a number of other consumer brands.

Fast Company A business magazine started in 1995 by two former Harvard Business Review editors, Fast Company focuses on innovation. It is now owned by Mansueto Ventures, which also owns Inc. The magazine publishes 10 issues a year.

featherbedding The practice of a union requiring a company to hire more workers than necessary to complete the work. **($$)**

Federal Aviation Administration A branch of the Department of Transportation that regulates the airline industry and airplane manufacturers. *FAA* is acceptable on second reference.

Federal Communications Commission The federal regulatory agency charged with overseeing interstate and international communications by radio, television, wire, satellite and cable. *FCC* is acceptable on second reference.

Federal Deposit Insurance Corp. The government arm that attempts to maintain stability in the financial market by insuring most bank deposits and examining financial institutions. *FDIC* is acceptable on second reference. Note that the FDIC prefers the word "chairman" before its head, Sheila Bair.

Federal Energy Regulatory Commission The agency that regulates natural gas and electricity transactions. *FERC* is acceptable on second reference.

federal funds rate The interest rate at which financial institutions borrow very short-term money from each other through the Federal Reserve Board. The Federal Open Market Committee sets a target for this rate, but the actual rate is determined in the open market. **($$$$)**

Federal Highway Administration A federal government agency that is part of the Department of Transportation and oversees the country's highways and roads. Do not use FHA on second reference.

Federal Home Loan Bank system A dozen regional banks throughout the country from which local lenders borrow money to fuel economic development and housing construction. It essentially brings the debt market to **Main Street**. The Home Loan Bank system is a government-sponsored enterprise chartered by Congress in 1932. Do not use FHLB on second reference. Refer to it as the *system* on second reference.

Federal Housing Administration A government entity that provides mortgage insurance to lenders it approves. *FHA* is acceptable on second reference.

Federal Open Market Committee The 12-person board that sets the country's monetary policy. It includes the seven members of the Federal Reserve Board and five presidents of regional reserve banks, one of whom is always the president of the Federal Reserve Bank of New York. Do not use FOMC on any reference. **($$)**

Federal Reserve Board The federal government agency that makes key decisions about short-term interest rates. The chairman is considered one of the most powerful people in the United States. On second reference, use the *Fed* or the *board*. Do not lowercase Fed on second reference.

Federal Trade Commission The federal agency that works to ensure the nation's markets are efficient and free of restrictions that harm consumers. The commission enforces federal consumer protection laws that prevent fraud, deception and unfair business practices. The commission also enforces federal antitrust laws that prohibit anticompetitive mergers and acquisitions and other business practices that restrict competition and harm consumers. *FTC* is acceptable on second reference.

FedEx Corp. Do not spell out Federal Express on any reference to the Memphis, Tenn.-based delivery service company.

Fiberglas A trademarked product. The generic term is fiberglass.

FICO score An individual's credit score that is used by lenders to determine whether to give the person a loan. It stands for Fair Isaac Corp., which created the system. *FICO score* is acceptable in all references. **($$)**

fighting the tape When an **investor** is taking an action — buying or selling — that is contrary to the rest of the market. It is similar to **contrarian** investing. **($$$)**

Financial Accounting Standards Board A seven-person board that is independent of the federal government and sets the accounting standards used by companies in reporting their financial performance. *FASB* is acceptable on second reference. When referring to one of the board's rules, use the abbreviation and the number, such as *FASB 157 requires companies to report the value of their assets at fair value.* **($$)**

financial adviser A person who offers financial advice and planning to individuals. They typically are paid via commissions, although some are paid fees.

financial analyst A person who performs financial analysis on investments for internal or external clients as part of his or her job. This person can also be called an *equity analyst, investment analyst, research analyst* and *securities analyst.* See **buy-side analyst** and **sell-side analyst. ($$$)**

financial derivative An investment whose value depends on the value of the underlying assets. See **derivative. ($$)**

Financial Institution Regulatory Authority A regulatory body that oversees brokers and dealers and their interaction with the investing public. It was created in 2007 by the merger of the New York Stock Exchange regulatory committee and the National Association of Securities Dealers regulatory apparatus. *FINRA* is acceptable on second reference.

financial landscape A phrase used in business journalism, often to describe a change, as in the *changing financial landscape.* This phrase has become overused and should be avoided because the world of finance and business rarely involves trees, bushes and shrubs.

financial planner A person who provides advice to individuals for situations such as funding for retirement and how to ensure descendants pay smaller estate taxes. This person differs from a **financial adviser,** who focuses on investing an individual's money. It is not to be confused with a stock broker, who is sometimes called a financial adviser.

financial porn A term first used by personal finance writer Jane Bryant

Quinn in 1998 to describe articles that encourage readers to make investment decisions that may not be wise, but will sell magazines or newspapers.

financial ratio A number of mathematical measures that help investors evaluate a company. These include everything from **return on equity** and **debt-to-capital ratio** to a **price-to-earnings** and **price-to-book ratio**. When writing about a financial ratio, refer to the specific one being used.

financial supermarket A financial services company that provides a wide range of the services an individual might need, from a checking account at a bank to a stock brokerage and insurance agency.

Financial Times, The A British-based business newspaper launched in 1888. It is considered a competitor to The Wall Street Journal, primarily in Europe, where it dominates.

firm Popularly, it can be used for any company. Technically, it applies to businesses of two or more people that are not legally recognized as a separate person, as is the case with corporations. It's commonly used when referring to law firms or accounting firms. The term firm is also used when a company is the subject of an acquisition, i.e. *target firm*.

FIFO An accounting method that assumes for purposes of calculating cost of goods sold that the first inventory in a warehouse is the first shipped out when orders are placed. It does not have to correspond with the actual physical flow of inventory. When materials prices are rising, FIFO makes earnings higher but also increases income taxes. The term *FIFO* stands for first in, first out and should be explained on first reference. **($$)**

fire To discharge or terminate someone from his or her job. In some instances, the employee has been fired for cause, meaning the employer believes the employee hasn't met required standards. *Dismissed* is also acceptable.

first-quarter, first quarter Hyphenate when used as a compound modifier, such as *a company's first-quarter earnings rose 23 percent.* No hyphen when it stands alone, such as *profits also rose in the first quarter.*

In earnings stories, avoid using the term quarter repeatedly. Other acceptable terms are *in the last three months* or *period.*

fiscal policy Government spending or taxing policies that influence the broad economy.

fiscal quarter, fiscal year The term fiscal is not necessary except on first reference when referring to a fiscal year that does not coincide with the calendar year. Simply use *quarter* and *year* instead.

Fitch Ratings A credit rating agency based in New York and London, although its parent company is based in Paris. Its competitors are Moody's and Standard & Poor's. *Fitch* is acceptable on first reference.

501(c)(3) A provision of the U.S. Internal Revenue Service code that exempts certain types of organizations, such as charities, churches and universities, from paying federal taxes. These organizations are called **nonprofits**. Note that both the c and the 3 are in parentheses. **($$)**

fixed annuity An insurance contract in which the insurer makes a regular payment into the contract for its term. It's considered a safer investment than a **variable annuity. ($$$)**

fixed income A type of investing or budgeting strategy in which income is received at a regular rate. A fixed-income strategy is typically used by retirees or risk-averse investors. **($$)**

fixed-rate mortgage A mortgage where the interest rate will not change during the course of the mortgage. When writing about mortgages, distinguish between fixed-rate and adjustable-rate. **($)**

flack Derogatory term for public relations professionals. Do not use in print. **Spokesman, spokeswoman** or **representative** is preferable.

flak Slang for strong criticism. The term comes from anti-aircraft fire.

flash price The price of a stock that shows when trading is extremely heavy. The ticker will "flash" forward to the current price instead of reporting the incremental changes. **($$$)**

flash trading Where traders use computers to examine investors' orders for milliseconds before publishing them to the rest of the market, having bought or sold the shares first after analyzing the trade. The Securities and Exchange Commission moved in 2009 to ban such trading.

Fleishman-Hillard Co. Hyphenate the name of the St. Louis-based public relations agency.

flexible spending account A type of savings account in the United States where workers can set aside pre-tax money to pay for expenses such as health care or dependent care. Do not use FSA on any reference. **($$)**

flexible work schedule An alternative to the traditional 9 a.m. to 5 p.m., 40-hour work week, it's a policy at many companies that allows employees to adjust their work schedules, particularly their arrival and/or departure times. It's also known as an *alternative work arrangement.*

flipping An investing strategy where the individual buys an investment in the hope that it can be sold quickly at a higher price. Flipping became common in many real estate markets in the first decade of the 21st century. **($$)**

float The amount of stock available for trade in a company on a regular basis. The float is less than the total number of outstanding shares because of **restricted stock** given to executives and in some cases large blocks of stock held by holders who don't plan to sell. **($$$)**

flow of funds Data collected by the **Federal Reserve Board** that shows the flow of money in certain sectors of the economy, such as the lending of money by banks and investing in businesses. Flow of funds can also be used to refer to the movement of money into or out of a mutual fund or a specific stock. The data is released quarterly, typically on the first Thursday of the final month of the following quarter. The story focuses on domestic nonfinancial debt. **($$$$)**

FNB Bancorp A bank based in San Francisco, but F.N.B. Corp. is a bank based in Hermitage, Pa.

Food and Drug Administration A federal government agency that regulates the safety of food and pharmaceuticals, certifying when drugs can be sold to the public. It also regulates animal food, cosmetics, and medical devices, among other products. *FDA* is acceptable on second reference.

Sometimes wrongly called the "Federal Drug Administration," which doesn't exist.

forecast A term used to describe when a company predicts future earnings or other financial performance. Avoid using when describing an analyst's prediction for a company's financial performance. *Estimate* is preferable when referring to an analyst.

foreign exchange trading The buying and selling of various currencies. The foreign currency market is the largest in terms of value traded daily. When writing about foreign exchange trading, the values of currencies should always be paired. For example, the value of the U.S. dollar should be compared with the British pound, or the Japanese Yen should be compared with the **euro**. In general, stronger-than-expected U.S. economic data is positive for the U.S. dollar in foreign exchange trading, and vice versa.

forensic accounting A term to describe using auditing and investigative tactics to examine a company's financial statements. Some business journalists turn to forensic accounting experts to help them determine the true finances of a company. **($$$)**

Forbes A business magazine started in 1917 by Bertie Charles Forbes, Forbes remains primarily in the hands of the Forbes family, although a minority stake was sold in 2006. Forbes is best known for its lists, including the Forbes 400 list of the richest people in the United States. It is the longest-running business magazine in the United States.

Form 3 A document filed with the Securities and Exchange Commission by an insider of a company or someone who owns more than 10 percent of the company's stock. It must be filed within 10 days of the person becoming an insider or the investor passing the 10 percent threshold. See **insider.**

Form 4 A document filed with the Securities and Exchange Commission by a company insider or an investor with more than 10 percent of the company stock when the amount of stock he or she owns changes, either through a purchase or a sale. The document must be filed before the end of the second business day after the trade.

Form 8-K A document filed by public companies with the Securities and Exchange Commission when they have a materially important event occur. The SEC has a number of incidents that require the filing of an 8-K, including change of control, the resignation of a board member, the change in a fiscal year and change in auditors. Some companies include important earnings supplements in 8-Ks.

Form 10-K An annual document filed by all public companies and some private companies with the Securities and Exchange Commission at the end of their fiscal years. Companies must file this document within 60 to 90 days after the end of the fiscal year, depending on the size of the company. The 10-K includes the company's financial performance for the year as well as management's discussion of that performance.

Form 10-Q A quarterly document filed by all public companies and some private companies with the Securities and Exchange Commission at the end of each of their first three fiscal quarters. It is filed within 40 to 45 days after the end of the fiscal quarter and includes the most-recent quarter's financial performance. The company has typically already released this financial information in the form of an earnings release, but the 10-Q should still be reviewed to see if the company has added other information.

Form 990 A public document filed by nonprofit organizations with the **Internal Revenue Service**. A Form 990 must be filed within six months after the end of the fiscal year, and it includes how the nonprofit spent its money as well as the salaries for the top five employees. The Form 990 of a religious organization is exempt from public records requirements.

Form NT A document filed by a company when it is unable to file its Form 10-K, Form 10-Q or other filing with the Securities and Exchange Commission before the prescribed deadline. The Form NT is often, but not always, a sign that a company faces financial issues.

Form S-1 A document filed by a company with the Securities and Exchange Commission when it intends to sell shares to public investors. The S-1 is often amended with additional information before the shares are actually sold.

Form S-4 A document filed by a public company with the Securities and Exchange Commission in the event of an acquisition or merger. As a result, Form S-4s often have useful information about the deal, such as behind-the-scenes negotiations between the two companies, whether the price was raised or lowered, and whether there were competing bids.

Formica A trademarked product. The generic term is laminated plastic.

Fortune A business magazine started in February 1930 by Time magazine founder Henry Luce. It was published monthly until January 1978, when it became an every-other-week publication. The magazine spells its names with all capital letters, but lowercase all except the F.

Fortune 500 Commonly used to refer to a company that is listed in Fortune magazine's annual list of the largest companies in the United States. The list is based on the previous year's revenue.

foundation A nonprofit organization that donates funds to support other organizations. Foundations are required to spend at least 5 percent of their assets annually. Many of the largest U.S. companies — or their founders — have affiliated foundations. An example is the Bill and Melinda Gates Foundation, run by the co-founder of Microsoft and his wife.

401(k) plan A retirement plan available in the United States where workers can deduct a portion of their pay and have that money placed in a retirement savings plan. With a 401(k) plan, the worker then chooses how that money will be invested — mutual funds, company stock, money market accounts, etc. Note that the k is lowercase and always in parentheses. **($)**

Fox Business Network A cable business news television network started by News Corp. in October 2007 as a competitor to CNBC. Acceptable to use *Fox Business* on second reference. Lowercase the letters in Fox although the network spells it with all capital letters.

fractions When used, they should be spelled out, such as *three-fourths* or *four-fifths*. Decimals, however, are preferred in many business references, particularly stock prices.

franchise A license agreement between a company and a party that gives the party access to the company's operating techniques and trademarks in return for a start-up cost and an annual fee. Many restaurant companies, such as McDonald's and Burger King, operate using the franchise system.

Freddie Mac A shortened name for the Federal Home Loan Mortgage Corp., a government-sponsored enterprise that purchases and securitizes home loans. *Freddie Mac* is acceptable in all references.

free cash flow A measure of operating performance of a company. It is calculated by subtracting **capital expenditures** from a company's operating cash flow, which is **net income** adjusted for noncash items that affect income such as **amortization** and **depreciation**. Some companies create their version of free cash flow that differs from the customary definition. Always ask for how it is determined. **($$$)**

Freeport-McMoRan Copper & Gold Inc. Maintain the capitalization in McMoRan for the Phoenix-based mining company.

Freon A trademarked type of refrigerant whose use is being phased out because of concerns of its effect on the ozone layer. The generic term is refrigerant.

friendly takeover When a company's executives and board agree to sell the operation to another company. It's in contrast to a **hostile takeover**, which is when a company makes an offer to buy another company after the target rebuffs an acquisition offer. **($$)**

Frisbee A trademarked product. The generic term is flying disk.

front running (n.) An unethical practice in which a broker trades in a stock based on information from his firm's research department or trading desk before it is given to clients. For example, a broker might acquire 100 shares of a company just before the research department issues a "buy" rating on the stock, which would result in the firm's clients also buying the stock, sending the price higher. **($$$$$)**

Fudgsicle A trademarked product. The generic term is fudge ice-cream bar.

fund A collection of money from various investors into a large pool, which then invests that money uniformly, such as a mutual fund or a hedge fund.

fund of funds A mutual fund or hedge fund that invests its money by investing in other mutual funds or hedge funds. **($$)**

fundamentals Qualitative and quantitative information that contributes to the value of a company or an investment.

futures A contract that requires the buyer to purchase an asset at a predetermined future price and date. A futures contract can be purchased for a stock or a commodity. Such contracts lock in the price for the investor, minimizing the risk of the price going up or down. **($$$)**

G-5 Otherwise known as the Group of Five, the top five industrialized countries in the world that meet regularly to discuss economic and monetary issues. The countries are France, Germany, Japan, the United Kingdom and the United States. *Group of Five* is acceptable on first reference, while *G-5* is acceptable on second reference. **($$$$)**

G-7 Otherwise known as the Group of Seven, it includes the Group of Five countries plus Canada and Italy. It deals primarily with economic issues. *Group of Seven* is acceptable on first reference, while *G-7* is acceptable on second reference. **($$$$)**

G-8 Otherwise known as the Group of Eight, it includes the Group of Seven countries plus Russia. *Group of Eight* is acceptable on first reference, while *G-8* is acceptable on second reference. Reuters refers to these countries as the *world's richest countries* on second reference. That's acceptable as well. **($$$$)**

gadfly An investor who attends a company's annual meeting and often asks embarrassing questions to its management. The term is acceptable, as many gadflies revel in their role. The most famous is Evelyn Y. Davis.

gas vs. gasoline While it may be OK to use *gas* on second reference as a synonym for *gasoline* (what most of us use to fuel our cars), make sure there's no confusion with other fuel gases, such as natural gas or propane, which also can power vehicles and are becoming more commonly used. Best practice is to use *gasoline* on first reference except in casual uses: *He ran out of gas*. Never refer to diesel fuel as gas.

gas, natural The common home-heating fuel, delivered by pipelines. Always use *natural gas* on first reference. See also, **Natural gas pricing.**

Geico Capitalize only the first letter in the name of the auto insurer, in contrast to the all caps that the company uses. Geico is now a subsidiary of Berkshire Hathaway Inc. Its headquarters is in Chevy Chase, Md., although its corporate address is Washington, D.C.

General Electric Co. A conglomerate based in Fairfield, Conn. *GE* is acceptable on second reference.

General Motors Co. An automaker based in Detroit. *GM* is acceptable on second reference. General Motors Corp. was the name of the company before filing for bankruptcy court protection in 2009.

generally accepted accounting principles A common set of accounting standards and procedures used by companies to compile their financial statements. Reporters should always be leery of management that responds, "It's GAAP." Some managements are more aggressive than others in their interpretation. *GAAP* is acceptable on second reference.

general obligation bond A municipal bond issued based on the credit rating and taxing power of the government entity rather than just the revenue that would be generated from the project that will be constructed from the money raised by the bond issue. General obligation bonds are usually used to fund projects such as roads and parks that don't produce revenues. Do not use GO bond on second reference. **($$$$)**

Glass-Steagall Act The act passed by Congress in 1933 that prevented commercial banks from owning brokerage firms or investment banks. It was repealed in 1999. As a result, it is rarely mentioned in current business news stories.

GlaxoSmithKline PLC The name of the London-based pharmaceutical company is all one word. *GSK* is acceptable on second reference.

going concern A description used for a company that has the financial resources to continue operating indefinitely. **($$)**

golden handcuffs Long-term incentives promised to employees or executives so that they will remain with the company. The employee often forfeits the incentive if he or she leaves the company. **($$$)**

golden parachute Lucrative benefits given to top executives in the event their company is taken over by another firm, resulting in the loss of a job. These benefits could include **stock options,** bonuses and severance pay. **($$$)**

goodwill When one company is purchased for another company above the value of its tangible assets, the difference is called goodwill. Goodwill comes from intangible assets such as the value of a company's brand names or its customer list. **($$$)**

Google Inc. The formal name of the Internet-search company includes Inc. When referring to its search function, do not use Google as a verb.

Government National Mortgage Association Otherwise known as Ginnie Mae, it's a federal entity that guarantees the payment of loans backed by the Federal Housing Administration, the Veterans Administration or Rural Housing Service. *Ginnie Mae* is acceptable on first reference.

government-sponsored enterprise A privately held corporation created to lower the cost of lending and capital in the economy. Examples are Freddie Mac and Fannie Mae. Do not use GSE on any reference. **($$$)**

grantor trust A trust where its maker retains control of the management of the trust and the distribution of its assets. **($$$)**

Great Depression The decade-long recession that began in October 1929 with the crash of the U.S. stock market. The *Depression* is acceptable on second reference.

greenmail A strategy where an unfriendly investor purchases a large amount of stock in a company, forcing the company to buy back the stock at a higher-than-market price to prevent a takeover. **($$$)**

Greenspan, Alan Chairman of the Federal Reserve Board from 1987 to 2006. Greenspan oversaw the longest economic expansion in U.S. history, but some of his policies are being criticized as leading to the recession that began in 2008. Greenspan's relationship with the business media was characterized by giving off-the-record interviews and being the subject of a number of laudatory articles.

greenwashing The act of promoting environmentally friendly measures or images but actually operating in a way that harms the environment. **($$$)**

gross domestic income The sum of all income in the production of goods and services in an economy. It differs slightly from **gross domestic product**. *GDI* is acceptable on second reference. **($$)**

gross domestic product The value of all goods, services and products by an economy during a certain time period. It includes purchases, investments and exports minus imports. Stories about the gross domestic product focus on the annualized quarterly percentage change in the GDP. *GDP* is acceptable on second reference. **($$)**

gross margin Revenue minus cost of goods sold divided by revenue. It measures the money a company makes on its product or service before paying for other expenses. Gross margins can vary by industry. **($$)**

gross national product The measure of all output produced by a country's residents and resident-owned capital, regardless of where that output is produced. For the United States, it would include output produced by residents and capital abroad, but exclude output produced by foreign-owned capital and foreign residents produced in the United States. The difference between gross domestic product and gross national product in the United States is small, but it can be large in other countries. *GNP* is acceptable on second reference. **($$)**

gross profit Revenue minus cost of goods sold for a company. It can also be called *gross income.* **($$)**

growth fund A mutual fund that attempts to invest in stocks of companies that are growing rapidly. **($$)**

growth stock A stock where the company's revenues and profits are expected to grow at a faster rate than competitors'.

guaranteed investment contract An insurance contract that promises the holder the repayment of the principal plus interest for a predetermined time period. **($$$$)**

Guess Inc. Do not use the question mark in the name of the Los Angeles-based company.

H&R Block Inc. Use the ampersand in the name of the Kansas City, Mo.-based tax preparer.

hard money Money borrowed from a nonregulated lender. Hard money loans are typically for higher interest rates and for shorter time periods than traditional loans.

HarperCollins Publishers Inc. The name of the publisher, a subsidiary of News Corp. is one word with a capital C.

HCA Inc. Use capital letters for the name of the country's largest hospital operator, formerly known as Hospital Corporation of America.

headquarters The location where a company's executives and many other employees reside. Some companies call their headquarters by another name. Home Depot refers to it as a "store support center." However, *headquarters* should be used in all references as it means that the company has other operating locations. Do not use as a verb.

health care The treatment and management of an illness or injury. It's always two words except when spelled as one word as part of the name of a company. Do not use the term health care to describe health insurance, and vice versa.

health insurance Coverage that helps pay for the treatment and management of an illness or an injury. Many consumers receive health insurance through their employer.

health maintenance organization A managed-care form of health insurance where the insurer has contracts with physicians and other medical care providers, guaranteeing them a certain number of patients. In return, the health care providers charge a flat rate to patients. *HMO* is acceptable on second reference. **($$)**

hedge funds An investment vehicle typically offered to institutional investors and individuals with high net worths. Do not use interchangeably with **mutual funds**. Although both pool investments into one fund, hedge funds differ from mutual funds in that they do not advertise publicly for investors, and the manager typically gets a share of investors' profits, a share known as the carried interest, or carry. Frequently funds hedge their investment bets by buying some investments they believe will rise in value and buying some investments they believe will decline, but trying to make money off both. See **short selling**.

However, many hedge funds no longer split their investments this way, so the term "hedge" is actually a misnomer. When writing about hedge funds, avoid using adjectives such as "risky," "hazardous" or "unsafe." **($$$$)**

hedging Making an investment to decrease the risk of the change in value of an asset.

held at the opening When a stock cannot be traded when the market opens. This occurs for two reasons: 1. The company might be about to release major news, or 2. An imbalance exists between buy and sell orders. **($$$)**

herd mentality Refers to when a large group of investors moves the market up or down by following the crowd. The opposite would be **contrarian** investing.

Hertz Global Holdings Inc. The Park Ridge, N.J.-based company does not hyphenate the name of its Hertz Rent a Car subsidiary. It is also the parent of Advantage Rent A Car.

Hewlett-Packard Co. The Palo Alto, Calif.-based computer maker can be referred to as *HP* on second reference.

HH Gregg Inc. Capitalize the first two letters of the name of the Indianapolis-based electronics retailer, although the company uses lowercase letters.

high-yield bonds See **junk bonds.**

Hi-Liter A trademarked product. The generic term is highlighting marker.

hold A rating given a stock by a sell-side analyst who doesn't think the shares will underperform or outperform the overall market. The analyst is telling investors not to sell the stock, but also not to purchase any additional shares. The **neutral** rating means the same thing.

holding company A holding company holds controlling interests in stock of other companies. It usually exists for that purpose alone. See also **parent company.**

holding period The time during which an investment is held by an investor. A holding period is used to determine the investment's performance. An investment that rose 10 percent that was held for three months would have an annual return of 40 percent. **($$)**

Home Depot Inc. Avoid capitalizing "the" before the Atlanta-based company's name.

homeowners insurance Insurance purchased by the owner of a home to protect against loss or damage to the house and its contents, along with liability coverage. Two of the largest home insurers in the country are State Farm and Allstate.

hostile takeover An acquisition that occurs when the target company does not want to be sold. In some cases, the company making the offer will bypass the company's board and its management and make a pitch to shareholders. **($$)**

hot issue An **initial public offering** that trades well above the offering price on the first day of trading.

household survey One of the ways in which the unemployment rate is determined. Monthly interviews are conducted by the U.S. Department of Labor with 60,000 households.

housing starts The number of residential buildings that have begun construction in any month. The data includes construction starts and permits and is compiled by the Department of Housing and Urban Development. It is released around the middle of the following month. It does not include mobile homes, dorms, rooming houses or long-term hotels.

HSN Inc. The St. Petersburg, Fla.-based parent company of the Home Shopping Network.

hybrid fund A mutual fund that uses multiple investment strategies. **($$)**

hyperinflation Extremely high, out-of-control **inflation**. There is no quantitative measure for hyperinflation, so use the term carefully. **($$$$)**

IBM Acceptable on all references for International Business Machines Corp., which is based in Armonk, N.Y.

ICE Futures The current name of the New York Board of Trade.

Ikea Capitalize only the first letter in the name of the Swedish retailer instead of the all-capital spelling that the company prefers. The parent company is Inter Ikea Systems B.V.

illiquid An asset that can't easily be bought or sold at its current market price. **($$$)**

Imax Corp. Capitalize only the first letter in the name of the Toronto-based operator of large-screen movie theaters.

imbalance of orders Occurs when there are too many types of orders — buy or sell — for a specific stock to allow it to trade. *Order imbalance* is also accepted. **($$$)**

impairment When a company reduces the value of its capital because its assets are worth less than they are carried for on its financial statements. An impairment charge is generally not good news. **($$$)**

import and export prices A monthly index that measures the prices of goods imported into the United States and exported to other countries. It is measured by the Bureau of Labor Statistics and released monthly about the second week of the following month. The story focuses on import prices, particularly the monthly change in total and nonoil commodity prices.

Inc. A monthly business magazine founded in 1979 in Boston and now published in New York. The magazine owned by Mansueto Ventures is a sister publication to Fast Company. Inc. and is known for its list of the fastest-growing private companies in the United States, called the Inc. 5,000. Note that the period is always used in the magazine's name.

income Equals revenues less expenses. *Earnings* and *profit* are acceptable synonyms, but operating profit and operating income are not.

income statement The accounting of sales, expenses and net profit for a given period, such as a quarter or year.

income tax A tax levied by the government on the income of an individual, company or other organization.

incorporated An adjective indicating that a company or nonprofit organization is a corporation. Abbreviate as *Inc.* when used on first reference after the full company name.

incurred but not reported An accounting rule used by the insurance industry in which the cost of claims is estimated, but the actual claims have not yet been reported. This happens often after major hurricanes because insurance companies are unable to perfectly predict the value of their damage liabilities until all repairs have been made, which sometimes can take months or years. Do not use IBNR on any reference. **($$$$$)**

independent auditor An outside accountant with the Certified Public Accountant designation who inspects a company's financial statements.

index A collection of stocks or other securities that measures a change in a specific market. Examples of indexes are the Standard & Poor's 500 and the Dow Jones Industrial Average.

index fund A mutual fund that buys investments used in a specific index and tries to mimic the index's performance. It's considered a passive form of investing. **($$)**

individual retirement account A retirement account where people can invest money on a pre-tax basis and let it compound tax-free. Withdrawals from the account are taxable. *IRA* is acceptable on second reference.

inflation The increase in the prices of goods and services. When inflation rises, purchasing power falls. Inflation is measured by the **consumer price index**. **($$)**

informal inquiry A term used by the Securities and Exchange Commission when it collects information from a company to determine whether it should launch a formal investigation of potential wrongdoing. A company will often disclose an "informal inquiry" in its SEC filings. **($$)**

initial claims A number compiled by the Department of Labor that measures newly unemployed individuals who filed for unemployment insurance benefits in a given week.

initial public offering When a private company sells shares to the public for the first time and becomes a public company. Companies typically try to make their initial public offering when the market is receptive to investing in stocks of similar companies. *IPO* is acceptable on second reference.

In-N-Out Burger Note the hyphenation and capitalization for the Irvine, Calif.-based restaurant company.

insider A person with knowledge or nonpublic information about a company. The word can be used to describe executives, employees, managers, board members and investors.

insider trading The buying and selling of a company's shares by board members, executives and others within the company. Despite the term's negative connotation, nearly all trading by insiders is perfectly legal. When the trader has inside information that's not disclosed to the general public, insider trading is illegal. **($$$)**

insolvent When an individual or a company can no longer meet its obligations or when liabilities exceed assets.

institutional investor An investor such as a mutual fund company or money manager. Institutional investors are considered long-term holders of the shares, so companies try to cultivate relationships with institutional investors. **($$)**

intangible asset A company asset that is not physical, such as trademarks, patents and brand names. The iPod brand name is an intangible asset for Apple. **($$$)**

interbank rates The interest rate charged on short-term loans between banks. The **LIBOR** is the most common interbank rate. **($$$$)**

interest The fee that an individual or company must pay when it borrows money. The interest rate is usually expressed as an annual number.

interest expense The amount a borrower has paid for borrowed money during a specific time period.

interest income The amount of money that an individual or a company receives from others that it has lent money to. It can also be used to describe interest received on accounts such as certificates of deposits or savings accounts.

interest rate The rate paid on money borrowed, or received on money lent if you are the lender. It is typically expressed as a percent. A $1,000 loan borrowed at a 6 percent annual interest rate means the person pays $60 a year in interest.

internal audit When a company conducts an internal investigation of its operations, its processes and its procedures to determine how it can improve itself. Internal audits are also conducted to ensure that a company is following government rules and regulations, as well as its own procedures. **($$)**

Internal Revenue Service The federal regulatory agency that collects taxes from businesses and individuals. The IRS also determines the tax status of a business and reviews documents to determine if a company such as a nonprofit is in compliance with federal laws. *IRS* is acceptable on second reference.

international fund A mutual fund that invests primarily in non-U.S.-based companies. **($$)**

International Monetary Fund An organization of 185 countries that promotes the stability of currency exchanges, trade and payment for goods and services. It often lends money to countries in need. *IMF* is acceptable on second reference. **($$)**

Internet The short term for the World Wide Web. It's always capitalized.

intraday trading The buying and selling of shares within the same day. An investment can be described as reaching a new high or low *in intraday trading* if it does not close at that high or low during the end of the day. **($$$)**

inventory The materials and goods that a company holds that are ready for sale to customers. A company's inventory is recorded on its **financial statement**. If the inventory level is rising, it could be a sign that the company is having trouble selling its products, or that it is getting ready to expand its operations.

inverted yield curve When the interest rates of long-term debt are lower than the interest rates of short-term debt of the same quality. **($$$$$)**

investment banker A person working for a financial institution that is in the business of raising capital for corporations and municipalities. Investment bankers do the grunt work behind **IPOs** and debt offerings.

investment banking vs. retail banking Do not use these terms interchangeably. An investment banker provides services to large companies, such as selling stock to investors in an initial or secondary offering or negotiating terms in a merger or acquisition. A retail banker offers services such as checking and savings accounts to consumers.

investor A person or company that owns an investment.

Investor's Business Daily A Monday through Friday business newspaper based in Los Angeles that was started in 1984 by investor William O'Neil. It was called Investor's Daily until 1991. Avoid using the IBD abbreviation.

involuntary bankruptcy When creditors file a plan to force a debtor into bankruptcy court protection. The debtor can protest and argue against the involuntary bankruptcy before the court. **($$)**

iPhone A trademarked product from Apple. The generic term is **smartphone**.

iPod A trademarked product from Apple. The generic term is digital music player.

irrational exuberance A term used by former Federal Reserve Chairman Alan Greenspan in 1996 to warn that the stock market might be overvalued. It has since become a common term used to describe people, companies or other investments that have gotten ahead of themselves in terms of growth, expansion or value.

Jacuzzi A trademarked product. The generic term is whirlpool bath.

January effect Describes a general increase in stock prices in the first month of the year, generally attributed to selling in December by investors who want to create tax losses to offset capital gains. **($$)**

J.C. Penney Co. Inc. A retailer based in Plano, Texas.

Jeep Use when referring to the Chrysler-made vehicle. Use jeep for military vehicles. Otherwise, use sport utility vehicle.

Jell-O A trademarked product. The generic term is gelatin dessert.

JetBlue Airways Corp. An airline based in New York. The B is always capitalized.

jobless claims A number reported weekly by the U.S. Labor Department to track how many people are filing for unemployment benefits. There are two numbers reported. The first is **initial jobless claims**, which tracks the number of people filing for unemployment benefits for the first time. The second is **continuing jobless claims**, which tracks people who have previously filed for benefits. When writing about these data, please distinguish between the two numbers. Jobless claims are reported by the Department of Labor weekly on Thursdays, with a five-day lag for initial claims and a 12-day lag for continuing claims.

Jockey shorts A trademarked product. The generic term is boxer shorts.

joint venture When two companies create a separate, new company and agree to share its profits, expenses and control. The new company must have equal ownership between the two companies, otherwise it cannot be called a joint venture.

Jos. A. Bank Clothiers Inc. The Hampstead, Md.-based men's clothing retailer abbreviates Joseph.

JPMorgan Chase & Co. No periods or spaces in JPMorgan, but the securities division is J.P. Morgan Securities Inc. The company is headquartered in New York.

junk bonds, high-yield bonds The term junk bonds is more commonly used and is preferable when referring to bonds issued by a company that has a low rating from a rating agency. Junk bonds are typically rated below BBB- by Standard & Poor's and below Baa3 by Moody's.

Because they are rated lower, they offer a higher interest rate, or yield, to investors, but more risk as well. Wall Street uses the term "high-yield bonds" as a euphemism to give the issues a more positive connotation. **($$$)**

just in time An inventory strategy where the materials needed to produce a finished good are delivered just as they're needed. A just-in-time inventory cuts down on the amount of goods stored in warehouses. Many companies shift to just in time during an economic slowdown. The shift trickles through to suppliers, often causing their inventories to swell. **($$)**

K&W Cafeterias Inc. There are no spaces between the letters and the ampersand of the Winston-Salem, N.C.-based cafeteria chain.

Keogh plan A tax-deferred pension plan available to self-employed individuals or unincorporated businesses. There is no u in Keogh. **($$$$)**

KFC Corp. Use all capital letters for the chicken restaurant chain, formerly Kentucky Fried Chicken, based in Louisville, Ky. The parent company is named Yum! Brands Inc., but drop the exclamation point in writing.

kickback A form of payment made to persuade an individual or company to make a decision. For example, a stock broker might provide a kickback of his or her commissions to an investor who frequently trades stocks with the brokerage. Kickbacks are sometimes illegal, so be wary of using this term, as it has negative connotations. **($$$$)**

kicking the tires A slang term used to describe when one company does preliminary research about buying another company. It should be avoided.

Kiplinger's Personal Finance A personal finance magazine started in 1947 and called Changing Times until 1991. It bought Individual Investor magazine in 2001, folding that magazine's subscriber list into its own. As with other family-controlled media companies, ensure your writing distinguishes between the publication and the family member. On second reference, this publication can be referred to as *Kiplinger's*.

Kitty Litter A trademarked product. The generic term is cat-box filler.

KKR & Co The New York buyout firm is no longer called Kohlberg Kravis Roberts & Co.

Kleenex A trademarked product. The generic term is tissue.

Kmart No hyphen or space in the name of the retailer now part of Sears Holding Corp.

Kool-Aid A trademarked product. The generic term is soft-drink mix.

Krazy Glue A trademarked product. The generic term is super adhesive.

Krispy Kreme Doughnuts Inc. The Winston-Salem, N.C.-based company spells doughnuts differently from rival Dunkin' Donuts in its name. *Krispy Kreme* is acceptable on second reference. *Doughnut* is the correct spelling for the deep-fried cake treat.

K-Swiss Inc. The Westlake Village, Calif.-based shoe company's name has a hyphen.

L

Laboratory Corporation of America Holdings *LabCorp* is acceptable on second reference for the Burlington, N.C.-based medical testing company.

labor force The total number of people, 16 and older, employed and unemployed in an economy.

lagging indicators An economic measurement that begins to change after the economy has already moved in that direction. **($$)**

Land O'Lakes Inc. No space between the apostrophe and Lakes in the name of the farmers cooperative based in Arden Hills, Minn.

Land Rover A trademarked product. The generic term is sport utility vehicle.

large cap A term used to describe a company with a market capitalization of more than $10 billion. *Big cap* is also acceptable.

Laundromat A trademarked name. The generic term is coin-operated laundry.

layoff When a company eliminates jobs because of economic downturns or corporate restructurings. Companies use many other terms to describe layoffs, including "reduction in force," "rightsizing," "downsizing," "eliminations," "workforce moderations" and "streamlining the workforce." All of these should be avoided. Layoffs usually don't reflect on an employee's job performance. *Firing,* however, has a different connotation and should be used carefully. Both layoffs and firings are *terminations.* Challenger, Gray and Christmas Inc., a Chicago-based firm, issues a monthly report on corporate layoffs. It comes out the second or third business day of the following month at 7:30 a.m. EST. The story focuses on changes from the previous month and the same month a year ago.

La-Z-Boy Inc. Hyphenate the name of the Monroe, Mich.-based furniture manufacturer.

lead underwriter The managing underwriter who maintains the books of securities sold for a new issue. The firm is also commonly known as the **book runner. ($$)**

leading indicators An economic measurement that begins to change before the economy moves in that direction. The Conference Board compiles a leading economic index, a composite of 10 economic indicators. It is released on the third week of each month. **($$)**

LEED A registered trademark of the U.S. Green Building Council for its certification program. The acronym stands for Leadership in Energy and Environmental Design. Acceptable on first reference. The council describes the program as "the nationally accepted benchmark for the design, construction, and operation of green buildings." **($$$$)**

Lego Group Capitalize only the L in the name of the Denmark-based manufacturer of children's toys, as well as the name of its stores.

lender A financial institution that makes loans.

letter of credit A letter from a bank that guarantees that a buyer's payment to a seller will be received on time and for the correct amount. It's often used in international transactions. **($$)**

leverage The use of borrowed money to increase the potential return on an investment, or the use of debt to finance a company's assets. **($$)**

leveraged buyout A strategy involving the acquisition of a company using borrowed money. The acquirer uses the acquired's assets as collateral for borrowing in hopes that the future cash flow of the acquired company will cover the loan payments and produce a healthy profit. *LBO* is acceptable on second reference. **($$$$)**

Levi's A trademarked product. The generic term is jeans.

liability A legal debt or obligation, including accrual obligations such as pension liabilities. Recorded on the balance sheet, current liabilities are debts payable within one year, while long-term liabilities are debts payable over a longer period.

LIBOR The London interbank offered rate; it's the rate at which banks in London can borrow money from other banks on a short-term basis. *LIBOR* is acceptable on second reference. **($$$$)**

life insurance A policy purchased by an individual or company that promises a payment if the person dies.

LIFO The last-in, first-out accounting method for inventory. The assets produced or acquired last will be treated as if they are sold first. *LIFO* is acceptable on all references. **($$$)**

limit order An order placed with a brokerage firm to purchase or sell a certain amount of shares at a certain price or better. Limit orders are often used with low-volume or highly volatile stocks. **($$$)**

limited A form of company where the equity put into the business has limited uses based on its charter. When used on first reference at the end of the company's name, it's abbreviated

Ltd. This is the equivalent of Inc. for some non-U.S. companies.

Ltd. Co. A business structure used in Canada and England in which shareholder responsibility for company debt is limited, usually to the amount that the shareholder has invested in the company.

limited liability company A business structure with corporation and partnership aspects. Often a business will become a limited liability company to receive the tax advantages of a partnership and the liability advantages of a corporation. *LLC* is acceptable at the end of a company name on first reference only.

LLC Stands for **limited liability company**, not limited liability corporation. It's a form of a business that limits the liability of the partners.

LLP An abbreviation for limited liability partnership. Acceptable on all references.

LinkedIn Corp. The Mountain View, Calif.-based company that operates a social networking site for professionals spells its name as one word.

liquidate To convert an investment or asset into cash by selling it, or the process of a company selling some or all of its assets to pay off creditors.

liquidity The ease with which an asset can be bought or sold. An asset with high liquidity is being frequently traded at a stable price.

listed security Securities that have been approved for trading on a specific exchange.

Little League Baseball A trademarked name. The generic term is youth baseball.

load fund A mutual fund that charges consumers a commission or a sales charge. The money goes primarily to pay the **broker** or **investment adviser** for his or her expertise in selecting the fund. See **no-load fund. ($$)**

loan When an individual or a company borrows money from a financial institution. The borrower agrees to repay the money, plus interest, over a certain time period.

loan loss provision When a bank sets aside money for loans that it believes might default. An increase in a loan loss provisions means that a bank's loan portfolio is decreasing in quality. **($$$)**

lock-up agreement An agreement between the underwriters of a company's initial public offering and the executives and board members of that company that prevents those insiders from selling the stock for a certain amount of time — as short as four months or as long as a year — after the **IPO**. When the lock-up agreement expires and those insiders sell their shares, the stock price typically falls because of the increase in available shares in the market. **($$$$)**

LoJack Corp. The name of the Westwood, Mass.-based company is one word with a capital J. When referring to its LoJack car security product, maintain the same capitalization.

long-term debt Loans and other obligations that are due to be repaid in more than a year.

long position Owning an investment with the expectation that it will rise in value. The opposite is a *short position*. The phrases *buying long* or *going long* can also be used. **($$)**

loose credit The act of making credit easy to obtain. The real estate market in the United States in the early 21st century was marked by loose credit terms from lenders.

loss When expenses total more than revenue or sales. Losses *widen* and *narrow*. Do not use the terms rise and fall.

Lucite paint A trademarked product. The generic term is acrylic paint.

Mace A trademarked product. The generic term is tear-gas spray.

Magic Marker A trademarked product. The generic term is felt-tip marking pen.

Main Street A term used to describe the investing public. It's often used in contrast to **Wall Street**, which is used to describe the collection of professional investment and financial experts who primarily work in New York.

management The people at a company who are in charge. They organize, plan and direct the company's operations.

management buyout When the executives of a company purchase a controlling interest from shareholders. The management often teams up with an outside investor, such as a leveraged buyout house, to complete such an acquisition. Do not use MBO on any reference. **($$$)**

margin In business terms, the difference between a product's selling price and the cost to produce the product. Margin can also refer to money borrowed to purchase an investment.

margin call A demand made by a broker that an investor using margin

place more money or securities into his or her account. This typically occurs when the account decreases in value. **($$$)**

market capitalization A company's stock market value. It is calculated by multiplying the number of outstanding common shares by the current market price of a share. The term *market cap* is acceptable on second reference. **($$)**

market maker A broker-dealer that holds an amount of shares in a company to make it easier for investors to buy or sell the stock. The term is often used as a firm *making a market* in a stock. **($$)**

market share The percentage of a specific business or product line that a company controls with its offerings. Coca-Cola and PepsiCo controlled more than 70 percent of the carbonated soft drink market in 2008. Coca-Cola had a 42.8 percent market share, while PepsiCo had a 31.1 percent market share, according to industry newsletter Beverage Digest.

MarketWatch.com A business news website founded in 1994 and acquired by Dow Jones & Co. in 2005. The W is capitalized in the name although it's spelled as one word. Since its content is exclusively online, use the .com as part of the name in all references.

markup The difference between the lowest offering price for a security and the price that a dealer charges a customer. The term can also be used as the difference in price of a product sold by a retailer from the retailer's cost to purchase the product.

master of business administration An advanced degree offered by a university's business school. *MBA* is acceptable in all references.

material event An occurrence at a public company that would require it to file a **Form 8-K** with the Securities and Exchange Commission. **($$$)**

material weakness A phrased used by an auditor to indicate that the company's controls in reporting its financials are defective and could result in a misstatement of its performance. **($$$)**

maturity date The date the borrower has to pay back the money it has borrowed through a bond issue or loan. **($$)**

McMoRan Exploration Co. Retain the capitalization on the R for the New Orleans-based oil and gas company.

Medicaid The federal and state health insurance program that provides medical care for low-income families.

Medicare The federal health insurance program that subsidizes health care for those 65 and older and those who are disabled and have been on Social Security for two years.

Men's Wearhouse Inc. Avoid capitalizing "the" before the name of the Houston-based men's clothing store chain, and note the spelling of *Wearhouse.*

merger When two companies combine to form a new company, and the shareholders of each company own about 50 percent of the new company. Rarely, if ever, are there true mergers, although companies will announce takeovers as "mergers." Be careful when using this word. The more appropriate word often is **acquisition** or **takeover**.

MetroPCS Communications Inc. The wireless provider based in Richardson, Texas, spells its name as two words, with PCS capitalized.

metropolitan statistical area A formal metropolitan area as determined by the U.S. Office of Management and Budget. It is used to compile census and economic data on a regular basis. *MSA* is acceptable on second reference.

mezzanine financing A hybrid combination of debt and equity financing. The lender can convert the debt to an ownership position in the company if the loan is not repaid in time or in full. The origin of the term comes from Italian architecture, where a mezzanine floor is built between two main floors. **($$$$$)**

Michaels Stores Inc. No apostrophe in the name of the Irving, Texas-based craft retailer.

microbusiness A business with fewer than 10 employees. The definition is the same in the United States and the European Union. Microbusinesses often operate out of the owner's house.

microcap A company with a market capitalization between $50 million and $300 million.

midcap A company with a market capitalization between $2 billion and $10 billion.

midsized business A business that has between 100 and 500 employees in the United States and between 100 and 250 employees in the European Union.

millage The amount per $1,000 of assessed value used to determine taxes on a piece of property. **($$$)**

MillerCoors LLC The Chicago-based joint venture between SAB Miller and Molson Coors is one word.

momentum investing An investment strategy that relies on current trends in the market to continue. An investor buys into stocks and commodities that have risen in price, believing

that they will continue to keep rising. **($$)**

monetary policy The regulation of money supply and interest rates by a central bank. In the United States, the Federal Reserve regulates money supply. The Fed submits a monetary policy report to Congress twice a year, and the Fed chairman testifies to the House and Senate in conjunction with the report's submission.

Money magazine A monthly publication from Time Inc. started in 1972 to complement Fortune, another Time business magazine. It focuses primarily on personal finance. The word magazine is lowercased.

money market The market where investments with high liquidity and short maturities are traded. They include Treasury bills, certificates of deposits and municipal notes.

money market funds Mutual funds that invest in short-term debt instruments. A money market account from a bank is different. It's a savings account in which banks pay the lowest interest rate they can get by with.

money supply The entire quantity of currency, loans and credit in an economy. **($$)**

monopoly A situation in which a single company controls a large portion of a market for a product or a service, often resulting in higher prices.

monthly Treasury statement A report from the U.S. Treasury Department that totals the revenues collected and the payments made by the federal government each month. It comes out about two weeks after the end of each month, and the story focus is on the overall surplus or deficit.

Moody's Corp. The New York-based parent company of Moody's Investors Service, which rates credit issues and provides financial research. Use Moody's on second reference for both.

Moon Pie A trademarked name. It should be capitalized. The generic term is marshmallow sandwich.

Morningstar Inc. A Chicago-based independent investment research company best known for providing information about mutual funds.

mortgage A loan used by an individual or company to purchase real estate. The loan is secured by the real estate purchased. The lender can take ownership of the real estate if the buyer fails to repay the loan.

mortgage application An application to borrow money to purchase property. Mortgage application data is released weekly on Wednesdays by the Mortgage Bankers Association of America. The story on the data focuses on changes in the purchase index, the refinancing index and the four-week moving average.

mortgage bank A financial institution that originates loans for real estate, funding them through its own funds or a **warehouse lender**.

motor vehicle sales The number of domestically produced cars, SUVs, vans and light trucks sold during a monthly time period. Car manufacturers report their sales on the first business day of the following month. Motor vehicle sales are less than 5 percent of the gross domestic product, but they are important because they are highly discretionary purchases and are looked at to see whether consumer spending behavior is changing. The latest data on new car sales is available at http://www.motorintelligence.com/m_frameset.html. The term *new car sales* is also acceptable.

Motors Liquidation Co. The name of the old General Motors Corp., which entered into bankruptcy court protection.

multiple A term used to describe a measure of a company's stock price. Both **price-to-book ratio** and **price-to-earnings ratio** can be referred to as a multiple after first reference. **($$)**

municipal bond Debt issued by a state, county or municipality to fund capital expenditures, such as roads and schools. Avoid using the term "muni." Municipal bonds can be both **general obligation bonds** and **revenue bonds**. **($$)**

municipal note A short-term municipal borrowing that matures in one year or less. **($$)**

mutual fund Fund operated by an investment company that raises money from shareholders and invests it in stocks, bonds, options, commodities or money market securities. Mutual funds are seen as a less-risky way for small investors to invest in the market. **($$)**

mutual ownership An ownership structure commonly found in the insurance and thrift industries where the company is owned by the policyholders and depositors. **($)**

MySpace.com Note the capitalization for the News Corp. division.

naked shorting The illegal practice of shorting a stock without actually having the stock to short. Short selling requires that the shares be borrowed before they are shorted. In naked shorting, the shares are not borrowed. **($$$$$)**

Nasdaq Created in 1971 as the world's first electronic stock market, the Nasdaq — which stands for National Association of Securities Dealers Automated Quotations — is a computerized system that facilitates trading and provides price quotations on about 5,000 of the more actively traded over-the-counter stocks. Its largest stocks include Microsoft, Dell and Cisco. Do not use all caps.

Nathan's Famous Inc. The name of the Westbury, N.Y.-based restaurant chain does not include hot dog.

National Association of Securities Dealers The former self-regulatory agency of the securities industry that also oversaw the Nasdaq exchange. In 2007, it merged with the New York Stock Exchange's regulation committee to form the **Financial Industry Regulatory Authority,** or *FINRA*.

National Bureau of Economic Research A private, nonpartisan research organization. *NBER* is acceptable on second reference.

National Credit Union Administration The federal agency that regulates credit unions in the country. *NCUA* is acceptable on second reference.

national deficit vs. national debt Do not confuse these terms. The national deficit is the annual budget deficit of the federal government. The national debt is the total amount of money owed to creditors of the federal government. These creditors own Treasury bills, notes and bonds.

National Labor Relations Board A federal agency created in 1935 to enforce the National Labor Relations Act. It conducts secret-ballot elections to determine whether employees want union representation and investigates unfair labor practices by employers and unions. *NLRB* is acceptable on second reference.

natural gas pricing Remember that *mcf* stands for 1,000 cubic feet, not a million (think Roman numerals). Gas sales can be in those units or in BTUs — British Thermal Units — a measure of the gas's heat content. *BTU* can be used on first reference, but usually explained elsewhere in the story; substitute *1,000 cubic feet* for *mcf* in all references, except publications serving the energy industry. **Additional terms:** A *therm is* 100,000 BTUs and a *dekatherm* is 10 therms.

Use *per million cubic feet*, not dekatherm, when natural gas is priced that way.

Naugahyde A trademarked product. The generic term is simulated leather.

NCR Corp. The Dayton, Ohio-based company's name is all capital letters.

negative equity When the value of an asset falls below the balance of the loan used to purchase the asset. The term *upside down* is also acceptable. The term can also refer to a situation where a company's liabilities exceed its assets. **($$)**

negotiated sale A municipal bond sale in which the government entity and an underwriter work together to set the terms of the sale rather than having underwriters bid on the offering to set the terms. It often results in a better rate for the issuer. **($$$$$)**

Neiman Marcus Group Inc. No hyphen in the name of the Dallas-based upscale retailer, and note the spelling of Neiman.

Nerf A trademarked product. The generic term is foam toy.

net asset value A mutual fund's assets per share or an exchange-traded fund's net assets divided by the number of outstanding shares. *NAV* is acceptable on second reference. **($$$)**

net income A company's total earnings, after subtracting costs of doing business, depreciation, interest, taxes and other expenses. Do not confuse net income with **net operating income**. When a company loses money, it's called a *net loss*. This is the most important number in any earnings story.

net interest income For financial companies, the difference between the interest received on loans and the interest it pays on deposits and other borrowed funds. **($$)**

net operating income A company's profits after operating expenses are subtracted, but before subtracting depreciation, income taxes and interest. The term is commonly used by banks, insurance companies and other financial institutions and is not part of **the generally accepted accounting principles**. *Operating income* is also common, as is *operating profit*. **($$)**

net proceeds The amount of money left over after all costs are deducted from the sale of an asset or securities, such as stock. In an initial public offering, the net proceeds are the money that a company raises after paying its underwriters and other expenses. **($$$)**

net worth The amount by which the value of an individual's or a company's assets exceeds liabilities.

neutral A rating given to a stock by a sell-side analyst. A "neutral" rating means that the analyst doesn't believe that the stock will outperform the overall market, nor will it underperform the overall market. The rating **hold** is synonymous.

new home sales The sale of newly built homes to buyers from builders. An increase in new home sales can be a sign of a growing economy. Compiled monthly by the Census Bureau, the data is released in the last week of the following month. The story focuses on the level and the monthly change in total sales. Revisions to the data can be extensive.

New York Board of Trade A commodities exchange that trades futures and options on products such as sugar, cotton, coffee and orange juice. It was renamed ICE Futures US in 2007 after it was acquired by the Intercontinental Exchange, or ICE. The name New York Board of Trade is still used by some media outlets, but **ICE Futures** is the preferred name. Avoid NYBOT.

New York Mercantile Exchange The largest commodity exchange in the world. There are two divisions. The NYMEX primarily trades contracts for oil, propane, natural gas, platinum and palladium. The COMEX primarily trades contracts for gold, silver, copper and the Eurotop 100 Index. Avoid NYMEX and COMEX in all references.

New York Stock Exchange The largest stock exchange in the country. It is responsible for setting policies and supervising the stock exchange and its member activities. The NYSE also oversees the transfer of members' seats on the exchange and judging whether a potential applicant is qualified to be a specialist. *NYSE, the stock exchange* or *exchange* is acceptable on second reference.

Nike Inc. Lowercase the name of the Beaverton, Ore.-based sporting goods company after the N.

no-load fund A mutual fund without a commission or a sales charge. No-load funds make money from management fees. **($$)**

noncore A part of a company no longer considered part of its main strategy.

nonperforming asset A loan, held by a financial institution, that isn't paying interest. Such loans have typically not had a payment in the past 90 days. Avoid NPA in all references. Also called a *nonperforming loan.* **($$$)**

nonprofit organization An organization created to provide a good or service to the community without a profit motive. Also called a **501 (c) (3)**, many nonprofit organizations receive more in donations and other revenues than they pay out in expenses. Also referred to as a **not-for-profit** organization.

nonrecurring charge An expense that only occurs once on a company's financial statement. Can also be called a *nonrecurring item* but not always an **extraordinary item**. Extraordinary items are a subset of nonrecurring items. **($$$)**

North American Free Trade Agreement A 1994 agreement among the United States, Canada and Mexico that eliminated a number of tariffs and charges to encourage free trade on the North American continent. *NAFTA* is acceptable on second reference.

not a going concern A statement made by independent auditors that raises doubts about the company's ability to function in the future. **($$$$$)**

note A short-term debt issue, usually with a maturity of five years or less.

not-for-profit Another way to describe a **nonprofit organization.** The term also is used by the Internal Revenue Service to describe activities that it regards as hobbies or sporting or recreational activities, rather than businesses. Losses from those activities cannot be used to offset other income.

Novocain A trademarked product. Use the term local anesthetic.

NRG Energy Inc. Use all capital letters for the first name of the Princeton, N.J.-based energy company.

numbers In general, follow the Associated Press rule and spell out numbers below 10 and use the numerals for 10 and higher. Some exceptions would be stock prices, which are always numerals, and interest rates or yields, which are always numbers. Monetary amounts are always numbers. Also, spell out numbers that begin a sentence, and when numbers are included in a company name, follow the company's style, such as 3M and 20th Century Fox.

Obamanomics A word used to describe the economic policy of U.S. President Barack Obama. Avoid using unless it's in a quote.

obligation bond A municipal bond used to secure a mortgage on a piece of property that can be liquidated. The face value of the bond exceeds the value of the property. The difference is often used to compensate the lender for closing and transaction costs. **($$$$$)**

Occupational Safety and Health Administration A federal agency whose job it is to enforce laws to ensure a safe and healthy workplace. *OSHA* is acceptable on second reference.

occupational titles Follow the AP Stylebook and lowercase them. They include stockbroker, dealer, broker, lender, financial adviser, analyst, manager and financial planner.

off-balance-sheet financing The way a company raises money that does not appear on the balance sheet, unlike loans, debt or equity that do appear on the balance sheet. Examples are joint ventures, research and development partnerships and leases rather than purchases of capital equipment. **($$$$$)**

offering price The price at which an offering is sold to investors by the underwriters. With initial public offerings, the **opening price** may be different from the **offering price. ($$)**

Office of Thrift Supervision The part of the U.S. Treasury Department that is in charge of regulating savings banks and savings and loans. *OTS* is acceptable on second reference.

OfficeMax Inc. The name of the Naperville, Ill.-based office supply store chain is one word.

offshore Used to describe bank accounts, investments or company operations located outside a country's boundaries, often for tax purposes.

one-time charge An expense that a company says won't be repeated. **($$$$$)**

open-end fund A mutual fund has no restrictions on how many shares it will issue. Most mutual funds are open-ended. **($$)**

opening bell The beginning of trading in a market. In the United States, that occurs at 9:30 a.m. EST.

opening price The price at which an offering begins trading on the first day. The opening price is not always the **offering price. ($$$)**

open shop A place of employment where a prospective employee does not have to join a union or pay union dues to keep a job. See **closed shop** and **union shop.**

operating expenses Expenses that occur in the normal course of a business, such as salaries, rent for buildings, research and development costs and advertising.

operating margin Calculated by dividing a company's operating profit by net sales.

option A contract between a buyer and a seller that gives the buyer the right to purchase a security at a certain date at a predetermined price. In return, the seller receives a payment. This is called a *call option,* in contrast to a *put option.* Stock options are also commonly used as part of an executive's compensation package. **($$$$)**

order An instruction by a customer to a broker to buy or sell a security, often at a specific price.

Oreo A trademarked product. The generic term is sandwich cookie.

Organization of Petroleum Exporting Countries An intergovernmental organization of 13 oil-producing countries founded in 1960. Its goal is to coordinate the pricing and supply of oil and maximize revenue for OPEC countries during the long-term. *OPEC* and *cartel* are acceptable on second reference.

organized labor Another term for workers who belong to a union.

Ouija A trademarked product. The generic term is fortunetelling board game.

outperform A rating given a stock by a sell-side analyst. An "outperform" rating is considered the second-highest rating for many brokerage firms, right behind a "strong buy" rating. It's equivalent to a **buy** rating in most cases.

outside director A member of the board of directors who is not a current or former employee of the company and derives no significant income from it. Regulators have been pushing companies to add more outside directors.

overbought A situation in which demand to purchase an asset increases its prices to levels beyond what should be supported by its fundamentals. The opposite is **oversold. ($$$)**

oversold A situation in which the price of an asset has fallen sharply to levels below its true value. The opposite is **overbought. ($$$)**

oversubscribed A situation in which the orders for shares of an offering exceed the number of shares available to be sold. Provide the specific amount in a story. **($$)**

over-the-counter The market where stocks or debt instruments trade via a dealer network and not an exchange. *OTC* is acceptable on second reference. **($$)**

overvalued A stock price that is not justified by its current **price-to-earnings ratio**, asset value or its earnings projections. The opposite is **undervalued. ($$$)**

overweight A rating given a stock by a sell-side analyst. An "overweight" rating is considered the equivalent of an **outperform** or a **buy**. It also refers to when a portfolio has a higher percentage of a stock or group of stocks than an index it's tracking, such as the S&P 500.

Pablum A trademarked product. The generic term is baby food. Tasteless, simplistic writing is *pablum.*

Paccar Inc. Capitalize only the first letter in the first name of the Bellevue, Wash.-based manufacturer of Kenworth, Peterbilt and DAF trucks.

PalmPilot A trademarked product. Note that it is one word. The generic term is digital planner or personal digital assistant. Avoid using the abbreviation PDA when referring to a specific product.

panic Wide-scale selling of an investment without regard for the price, and a disregard for the investment's fundamentals. **($$)**

par The face value of a bond, such as $1,000 or $10,000. For common stocks, the par value has no relationship to the market price.

parent company A parent company controls a subsidiary through stock ownership, but has operations of its own. General Electric is the parent company of NBC. Compare with **holding company.**

partnership An unincorporated business in which two or more people manage and operate the business. All of the owners are liable for the debts of the business.

patent A government designation that gives the holder the sole right to use the process, design or invention for a specified time period. In the United States, most patents last for 20 years.

payday lender A finance company that provides small, short-term loans to borrowers to cover expenses until their next paycheck, often at high interest rates. Payday lenders typically require a recent paycheck stub. **($)**

PayPal Inc. The eBay subsidiary spells its name as one word.

penny stock A stock that trades at a very low price or has a very small market capitalization. Penny stocks may trade for more than $1 a share, but they are considered highly speculative and generally trade in the **over-the-counter** market. **($$$$)**

pension plan A retirement plan where the employer sets aside money for the benefit of its workers and promises them a benefit based on salary and years of service. Also known as a *defined benefit plan.*

Pension Benefit Guaranty Corp. A part of the Department of Labor that guarantees the payment of certain pension benefits.

Pep Boys – Manny, Moe & Jack Use the full name of the Philadelphia-based auto parts retailer only on first reference. *Pep Boys* is acceptable on second reference.

PepsiCo Inc. The food and beverage company based in Purchase, N.Y. The C is capitalized in its name.

percent Always spell out. Do not use the % sign, except in headlines and in The Wall Street Journal and Fortune magazine or when your publication's style requires it. Numerals are also always used with percents.

percentage point The difference between two percents. A change in consumer confidence to 80 percent from 70 percent is a change of 10 percentage points. (The term is not interchangeable with percent. A change in consumer confidence to 80 percent from 70 percent is a change of 14.3 percent.)

per share earnings A company's net income, less preferred stock dividends, divided by the total number of outstanding shares. It's also called **earnings per share**, which is more common on first reference.

personal finance Advice to readers and viewers on matters related to investing, retirement, savings, and other money-related issues. Some publications, such as Money and Worth,

focus exclusively on personal finance coverage.

Petco Animal Supplies Inc. Capitalize only the first letter in the first name of the San Diego-based pet supply retailer, which is privately held.

Pier 1 Imports Inc. Always use the numeral when writing the name of the Fort Worth, Texas-based retailer.

Ping-Pong A trademarked product. Note the hyphen. The name of the game is *table tennis*.

Pink Sheets A daily publication from the National Quotation Board that lists the prices of **over-the-counter** stocks and their **market maker**.

pink slip A term that refers to being fired or laid off from a job. It comes from the former practice, now nearly extinct, of human resources departments putting pink pieces of paper in people's pay envelopes when they were terminated.

plain vanilla The basic version of a financial investment, such as an option or a bond. The opposite is an **exotic instrument**.

PLC An abbreviation for a public limited company based in the United Kingdom. Acceptable on all references. The German equivalent is AG, while the French and Spanish equivalent is SA. The Italian equivalent is S.p.A.

poison pill A strategy by a corporation to discourage a hostile takeover. Sometimes, a poison pill will allow existing shareholders to purchase more shares of company stock at a discounted price if an offer is made for the company. **($$$$$)**

Ponzi scheme A fraudulent investment scam. It provides returns to the early investors by giving them the funds that later investors put into the scheme, but collapses when the scheme runs out of investors. The term originated with Boston-based Charles Ponzi and came back into popularity with the scam run by Bernard Madoff. It's slightly different from a **pyramid scheme. ($$$$$)**

pooling of interests An accounting method commonly used in the past during the combination of companies after mergers and acquisitions. It is not a valid accounting method anymore. **($$$$$)**

Popeyes Louisana Kitchen A subsidiary of Atlanta-based AFC Enterprises. There is no apostrophe in the name. It formerly was Popeyes Chicken & Biscuits.

Popsicle A trademarked product. The generic term is flavored ice on a stick.

portfolio A term used to describe a group of financial assets, such as stocks, bonds and commodities, managed by an investor, fund manager or a financial planner. Describe the investments instead of using the word portfolio.

portfolio manager A person who invests a mutual fund's assets.

POS An acronym commonly used in retailing that stands for point of sale. It refers to where the transaction occurs, and can also be used as an adjective for in-store advertising. *POS* is acceptable on second reference.

Post-It A trademarked product. The generic term is self-stick note.

PowerBar A trademarked product. Note that it is one word. The generic term is energy snack.

pre-existing condition An illness or medical condition that is excluded from coverage in a health or life insurance policy, either permanently or until a certain time period elapses.

predatory lending Providing loans to individuals who can't afford the monthly payments or understand the terms of the loan, which may have high interest rates or high fees. A company making such loans is called a *predatory lender*. The term comes from creatures that prey on other creatures. **($$$)**

preferred provider organization A managed-care plan similar to a **health maintenance organization** in which the patient can pick the physician and health care provider he or she wants as long as they are in the health insurance company's "preferred provider" network. The PPO enrollee will pay higher rates to receive health care from providers outside the network. *PPO* is acceptable on second reference. **($)**

preferred stock Shares issued in a company where the owner has more rights than the owners of regular, common stock. The preferred stock may require that it be paid a dividend before the common stock receives a dividend. However, preferred stock usually does not have voting rights. *Preferred shares* is also acceptable. **($$$$)**

pre-market trading Trading that occurs before the exchanges open.

premium The difference between the actual cost for acquiring a target firm versus its value before the acquisition.

prepackaged bankruptcy A situation where a company and its significant creditors agree to a reorganization plan before the company files for bankruptcy court protection. **($$$$$)**

president The officer responsible for the day-to-day management of a company who usually reports to the **chief executive officer**. This person is often called the **chief operating officer** as well.

price target The price a **sell-side analyst** believes a stock will reach within the next 12 months. The price target is usually listed on the front page of a **research report. ($$)**

price-to-book ratio Used to compare a stock's market value with its book value, calculated by dividing the current closing price of the stock by the most recently available book value per share. *P/B* is acceptable on second reference. **($$$)**

price-to-earnings ratio A stock analysis statistic in which the current price of a stock is divided by the company's earnings per share. *P/E* is acceptable on second reference. **($$$)**

Priceline.com Inc. Capitalize the name of the Norwalk, Conn.-based online company. The company lowercases the P.

PricewaterhouseCoopers LLP The name of the London-based accounting firm is all one word.

prime rate The interest rate that banks charge their most creditworthy customers, such as large corporations.

principal This word has a number of different meanings when writing about business. It could mean: 1. The amount owed on a loan, minus interest; 2. The original amount invested; 3. The face value of a bond; or 4. An owner of a public or private company.

private company A business whose ownership is confined to a handful of people, or whose ownership cannot be traded on a stock exchange.

private equity fund Typically a limited partnership that makes investments in companies, sometimes private, with the idea of selling the company in five to seven years for a higher price. Such funds are operated by *private equity firms*. A private equity fund is a Wall Street euphemism for "leveraged buyout fund." **($$$$)**

private placement The process by which a company raises money by selling stock to a small number of investors, such as insurance companies, pension funds and large banks. The stock is not registered with the Securities and Exchange Commission. **($$$)**

privately held A company whose shares are not traded on an exchange or through a dealer network. The company's shares may be held by one person, a group of shareholders, or employees.

Procter & Gamble Co. The consumer goods company based in Cincinnati is often misspelled as Proctor. *P&G* is acceptable on second reference. *Proctor-Silex* (note the "or") makes small kitchen appliances.

producer price index A measure of price change from the perspective of the seller, it measures selling prices for goods and services and is compiled by the Bureau of Labor Statistics. The data is released about two weeks after the end of the month, and the story focuses on the monthly percentage change. Use *index* on second reference. Do not use PPI on any reference. **($$$)**

productivity Output divided by input, with output being the goods and services produced and input being the number of worker hours. It's a measure of how the workforce is producing goods. The data is compiled by the **Bureau of Labor Statistics** and comes out about five weeks after the end of a quarter. The story focus is on the annualized quarterly percentage change in nonfarm business productivity, unit labor costs and compensation per hour. **($$$$$)**

pro forma A Latin term used to describe financial results that would have occurred given a merger, acquisition or other change in a company. When an acquisition is announced, the companies will typically provide pro forma financial numbers to show the combined operation's revenue and net income. **($$$)**

profit When revenue exceeds expenses and all other costs. **Income** is the preferred synonym.

profit margin Earnings after taxes divided by revenues. This is a number that is usually displayed as a percentage. Also referred to as the net profit margin. **($$$)**

profit-sharing plan A plan where the employees of a company share in its profits. The business typically decides what profits will be shared. **($$)**

profit-taking (n., adj.) A Wall Street euphemism for selling to take advantage of a sharp rise in price.

program trading Computerized trading that institutional investors use to execute large trades, typically when an index has reached a certain level. **($$)**

property and casualty insurance Insurance purchased by an individual or corporation that protects a business or property from loss. Auto and home insurance are examples. Do not use the ampersand when writing property and casualty. Avoid using P&C as well.

prospectus A document filed with the Securities and Exchange Commission when a company wants to sell stocks or bonds to investors. **($)**

proxy fight When shareholders or would-be acquirers try to force a change in control at a company. A proxy fight could be on the election of directors, the sale of a company, or the ouster of a **CEO**. *Proxy battle* is also an acceptable term. **($$)**

proxy statement A document sent to shareholders of public companies to invite owners of the company's stock to its annual meeting. The proxy statement will include information about proposals to be voted on at the annual meeting and executive salaries. It's formally known as a DEF 14A. Use the term *proxy statement* and not *DEF 14A*. **($$$)**

public company A business whose ownership interests, either shares or partnership units, are publicly traded.

public utilities commission State agencies that regulate water, natural gas, electrical and telephone companies. In some states, the agency may be called the *Public Service Commission*.

purchasing managers index An index compiled by the Institute of Supply Management and released on the first business day of the following month that measures new orders, inventory, supplier deliveries, production and employment at companies as a way to assess the health of the economy. The story focuses on the index and new orders. An index number above 50 means that the economy is expanding. *Purchasing managers index* is acceptable on first reference even though the Institute of Supply Management only uses PMI. *PMI* is acceptable on second reference.

pure play A company that has only one line of business, as opposed to a company that has different business lines. Coca-Cola is considered a pure play because it produces only beverages, whereas PepsiCo Inc. also has food businesses. **($$$$)**

put option A contract giving the holder the right, but not the obligation, to sell a security or property at a specific price within a certain time period. The buyer of a put is betting that the price of the equity will fall below the exercise price before the contract expires. **($$$$$)**

pyramid scheme An illegal investment scheme in which the initial members recruit new members, who must themselves recruit new members to receive a payment. The scheme collapses when not enough new members can be found. The difference between a pyramid scheme and a **Ponzi scheme** is that in a Ponzi scheme, the person running the scam does not ask the participants to find more members. **($$$$$)**

Q-Tips A trademarked product. The generic term is cotton swabs.

Quaalude A trademarked drug. The generic term is methaqualone.

quadruple witching When contracts for stock index futures, stock index options, stock options and single stock futures all expire at the same time. The day occurs on the third Friday of March, June, September and December. **($$$$$)**

Qualcomm Inc. Capitalize only the first letter in the first name of the San Diego-based cell phone manufacturer.

qualified opinion Suggests that the information provided was limited in scope or the company being audited did not maintain GAAP accounting principles. Contrary to its connotation, a qualified opinion is not a good thing. Auditors that deem audits as qualified opinions are advising that the audit is not complete or that the accounting methods used by the company do not follow GAAP. **($$$$$)**

quality of earnings A company with high quality of earnings typically has conservative accounting methods. *Earnings quality* is also a common term. The factors that can create low earnings quality include unusually low tax rates, a reversal of large reserves, a reduction in the allowance for doubtful accounts and share repurchases. **($$$$)**

quarter A three-month time period that acts as the basis for a company reporting its financial results. Do not abbreviate as Q1, Q2, etc., or as *in the first Q*. Quarter should be spelled out in all references.

quarterly services survey An **economic indicator** that the Census Bureau began collecting data for in 2003. It measures four services sectors: information; professional, scientific and technical services; administrative and support; and hospitals and nursing homes. Avoid QSS on all references. **($$$)**

quiet period The period of time during which the issuer of an offering cannot publicly issue any promotional statements or documents. Also known as the *waiting period*. **($$$)**

quitclaim deed A document in which one person disavows any interest in a piece of property and gives all rights to the property to another person. Such deeds are used in divorce cases, for example, where one person gives the sole rights to a home to the other. **($$$)**

RadioShack Corp. The Fort Worth, Texas-based retailer's name is one word.

raider An individual or company that tries to take over another company through a **hostile takeover.** Short for *corporate raider.*

rainmaker An employee or executive who typically brings in a lot of business to the company. Avoid unless it can be quantified. (**$$$$**)

raised Do not use to describe an increase in a dividend payment or in prices. Instead, say that dividends or prices *rose.*

rally A substantial increase in the value of stocks, bonds or equities, or an overall market, following a decline.

ranges Write $10 million to $15 million, not $10 to $15 million.

real dollars The price of a good or service adjusted for inflation. (**$$$**)

real estate investment trust A company that invests in real estate, either through property or mortgages, and must pay out virtually all its profits. *REIT* is acceptable on second reference. (**$**)

realized gain/realized loss The amount of money made, or lost, from selling an asset.

Realtor A trademarked name. The generic term is real-estate agent.

recapitalization The restructuring of a company's debt and equity in an attempt to make its capital structure more stable. A company issuing shares of stock to pay off some of its debt would be an example of a recapitalization.

receiver The person appointed by the bankruptcy court to run a company for a short period so that creditors will be repaid as much as possible.

recession A period of diminishing economic growth. Recessions are officially determined by the National Bureau of Economic Research's business cycle dating committee. The actual recession would have likely begun three to six months before it is declared.

record high/record low Terms used when a company's stock price, or the price of any equity, hits an all-time mark. Be careful to discern for readers the time element involved with the record. A stock that has hit a new high or low in the past 12 months is said to have reached a *52-week high* or a *52-week low*. The price of a barrel of oil hit an *all-time high* in 2008. Be careful, however, to figure in inflation when reporting commodity price records. Avoid using the terms high or low for equities if it's just within the past week.

recovery The end of a **recession** or **depression**, marked by renewed economic growth.

redemption The return of an investor's principal on a bond or preferred stock. A redemption occurs when the fixed-income security is paid off by the issuer. **($$)**

red herring A slang term used to describe when a company files a **prospectus** with the Securities and Exchange Commission because there is red lettering on the cover that states the company is not yet attempting to sell stock. **($$$)**

redlining The unethical practice by a financial institution of not doing business with customers who live in a low-income neighborhood. Redlining can involve mortgages or any other financial product, including auto and home insurance. **($$)**

Regulation Fair Disclosure A rule passed by the Securities and Exchange Commission in 2000 in an effort to prevent selective disclosure by public companies to market professionals and certain shareholders. *Regulation FD* is acceptable on second reference. **($$$$)**

reinsurance Insurance purchased by insurance companies to protect them from excessive losses on the policies they have written.

Rent-A-Center Inc. The Plano, Texas-based rental center operator hyphenates its name.

reorganization A process designed to revive a financially troubled or bankrupt firm. It typically involves the restatement of assets and liabilities in order to make arrangements for maintaining repayment. In some cases, the length of repayment terms is extended. Specify what the reorganization entails in a story.

repurchase agreement A form of short-term borrowing where an investor sells a security to a lender and agrees to buy back the security at a later date for a predetermined price. Do not use "repo agreement," but the *repo market* is acceptable on second reference to repurchase. **($$$$$)**

research and development Activities undertaken by companies to discover new products or business lines. Companies in technology and pharmaceutical businesses typically spend a lot of money on research and development. *R&D* is acceptable on second reference.

research note or **research report** Information compiled by a **sell-side analyst** and sent to the clients of the analyst's firm about a company's performance. A report is considered longer than a note. A research note or report will include the analyst's estimate of the company's future earnings, a recommendation on the stock and a 12-month target for the company's stock price, as well as a statement about whether the analyst holds the stock or the analyst's firm has done any investment banking for the company in question. The terms *note* and *report* are acceptable after first reference.

reserve Money theoretically set aside by a company from earnings to pay for other expenses, such as a pending lawsuit or other contingencies. It most cases, it is really just an accounting entry, as cash is not actually set aside.

restricted stock A restricted stock award is a grant of stock by an employer to an employee in which the employee's rights to the shares are limited until the shares "vest." Typically, the employee may not sell or transfer the shares of stock until they vest — frequently a defined period of time — and forfeits the stock if the employee's employment ends before the stock vests. **($$$$$)**

restructure General term for major corporate changes aimed at greater efficiency and adaptation to changing markets. A *restructuring* can be a sign that a company is having problems, but that's not always the case. This can also be called a *downsizing*, a *recapitalization* and a *major management realignment*. Specify what the restructuring entails.

restructuring charge A one-time expense that a company takes to reorganize its operations. A restructuring charge is typically related to the closing of plants or warehouses, or the writing down of the value of assets. **($$$$)**

results The financial performance of a company. Be more specific and write about earnings or losses.

retail sales The sale of retail goods, as compiled by the Department of Commerce, on a monthly basis. The data is released two weeks after the end of the month, and it breaks down sales into various categories, including food and beverage and auto, the most volatile sales number.

retained earnings The profits that a company retains after paying dividends. Retained earnings are listed on a company's balance sheet. **($$$$)**

return on equity A measure of a company's profitability calculated as net income divided by shareholder's equity. *ROE* is acceptable on second reference. **($$$$$)**

return on assets A measure of profitability for a company. It is calculated by dividing a company's net income by its assets. The number is a percentage, and the higher the percentage, the more profitable a company's operations are. *ROA* is acceptable on second reference. **($$$$$)**

return on investment A performance measure for an investment. It is calculated by subtracting the cost of an investment from the gain of an investment, and dividing that sum by the cost of the investment. If an investor purchased a stock for $10, and it was now worth $15, the gain would be $5. The difference between the cost and the gain is also $5. Dividing that number by the original cost gives a return on investment of 50 percent. *ROI* is acceptable on second reference. **($$$$$)**

Reuters A general news service that has a major business news component founded in Europe in 1851 by Paul Julius Reuter. It is now a subsidiary of Thomson Reuters. When referring to the parent company, use *Thomson Reuters* as two words. When referring to the wire service, use *Reuters.*

revenue The amount of money that a company receives or will receive for the sale of its goods and services, by renting goods or property, and through investment. The term *sales* cannot be used as a synonym because not all revenue is sales.

revenue bond A municipal bond that is payable only from the revenue of a project, such as a toll road or a stadium. **($$$)**

revenue recognition A determination when a company can record money it receives or will receive from the sale of a product or service as revenue. A company whose products experience a high return rate that cannot be estimated may have to wait a certain time period before it can recognize the sale as revenue. **($$$$$)**

reverse stock split A reduction in the number of outstanding shares of a company in an attempt to boost its stock price or its **earnings per share.** For example, a 1-for-2 reverse stock split means a shareholder owning two shares of a stock will now own only one. The stock price doubles, but the shareholder has half as many shares. A company will employ such a tactic sometimes when it is in danger of being de-listed by an exchange for having too low a stock price. **($$$$)**

reverse takeover A strategy used by a private company to become a public company without having to go through the **initial public offering** process. The private company buys enough shares of the public company to gain control, and then the shareholders of the private company exchange their shares for shares in the public company. Can also be called a *reverse merger* or *reverse IPO.* **($$$$$)**

revolving credit A line of credit where the customer pays a fee and then is allowed to use the money, up to a limit set by the bank, whenever it is needed. Can be referred to as a *revolver* on second reference. **($$$)**

right-to-work state States that prevent unions and companies from having an agreement that requires a worker to belong to the union to be employed. Right-to-work states are primarily in the South and Southwest. **($$)**

rights offering When a company issues rights that give holders the ability to buy additional shares of stock, typically at a discounted price. **($$$$)**

risk The concept that the return on an investment may not be the same as the investor's expectations. High-risk investments could cause investors to lose all their money, but they could also result in oversized returns.

risk capital The money that an investor places in risky investments.

roadshow When investment banks and executives of a company going public visit potential investors in an attempt to persuade them to purchase shares in the offering. The term **dog-and-pony show**, although a synonym, should be used sparingly. **($$$)**

robber barons A term that became popular in the late 19th century to describe businessmen who used unethical business tactics to amass large fortunes. John D. Rockefeller and J.P. Morgan were examples of robber barons. Today, the term has only the rare usage.

Rollerblade A trademarked product. The generic term is in-line skates.

Rolodex A trademarked product. The generic term is address-card file.

Roth 401(k) An employee-sponsored savings account that is funded with after-tax money. A Roth 401(k) plan allows the individual to begin withdrawing the money tax-free at age 59 and a half.

runoff The posting of the end-of-the-day stock prices for every stock on an exchange.

Russell 3000 Index An index that measures the performance of **small-cap** stocks.

Rust-Oleum A trademarked product. Note the hyphenation and capitalization. The generic term is moisture-resistant paint.

S

SA See **PLC** entry.

SABEW The *Society of American Business Editors and Writers*, located at Arizona State University. Acceptable to use *SABEW* on second reference.

S corporation A company that has met the requirements under subchapter S of the Internal Revenue code, allowing the company to be taxed as if it were a partnership. These businesses must be domestic, have 100 or fewer shareholders, and only one class of stock.

salary Payment given to employees at regular intervals in exchange for the work they have done. Traditionally, a salary is a form of remuneration given to professional employees on a monthly basis. When writing about executive compensation, salary is but one part. Focus on the total compensation package of an executive, not just the base salary.

sale The disbursal of a good or service by a company in exchange for money. The term *sales* cannot be used as a synonym for **revenue.**

sales per square foot A measure of a retailer's performance. It is calculated by dividing the retailer's total sales, or often revenue, by the total amount of square feet in its stores.

Jewelry stores typically have the highest sales per square foot, while book and sporting goods retailers have the lowest. Compare a retailer's sales per square foot of the current quarter with the same quarter last year to determine whether the retailer has improved its performance. **($$)**

same-store sales A measurement of the strength of a retailer's locations. Same-store sales compares the sales of stores open at least a year. A retailer can increase its overall sales by opening new locations, but if the same-store sales are declining, that means that its locations open more than a year aren't selling as much merchandise as they did during the first year of operation. Same-store sales are written about as a percent: *Same-store sales for Target rose 3 percent during the third quarter.* **($$)**

S&P 500 The Standard & Poor's 500 Index is considered one of the best barometers of the overall U.S. stock market. It should be considered as the stock index that provides the most accurate gauge for readers. *S&P 500* is acceptable on all references.

Sam's Club Capitalize only the first letter in the first name of the warehouse division of Wal-Mart Stores Inc.

Sandler O'Neill & Partners LP Use an ampersand, not a plus sign, in the name of this New York-based boutique investment bank.

Sanyo Electric Co. Capitalize only the first letter in the first name of the Japanese-based electronics manufacturer.

Sarbanes-Oxley Act A set of regulations passed by Congress in 2002 in an attempt to protect investors from fraudulent companies. The act requires company executives to sign off on their financial statements, and calls for stricter disclosures and harsh enforcement action. Do not refer to it as *SOX* on any reference.

savings and loan A financial institution that focuses on deposits and originating home mortgages with access to low-cost funding from the **Federal Home Loan Bank** system. Savings and loans, also known as *thrift banks,* have a community focus. *S&L* is acceptable on second reference.

Schedule 13D A form filed by any party acquiring an ownership of 5 percent or more of any equity registered with the SEC. The form must also be filed with the exchange on which the stock is traded. A Schedule 13D filing may indicate an investor who wants to make a change at the company — with its management, its board or its overall strategy — but most investors who file the document are simply taking a big stake in the company.

Schedule 13G A form filed by any party acquiring a beneficial ownership of 5 percent of more of any equity registered with the SEC. The difference between it and a **Schedule 13D** is that the filer of a Schedule 13G is considered a passive investor, like a mutual fund, that does not seek to exert control on the company.

Scotch tape A trademarked product. The generic term is cellophane tape.

seat A term used to indicate membership in the New York Stock Exchange.

second mortgage A subordinated mortgage made on property while the original mortgage is still in effect. The original mortgage has first claim on the property. A second mortgage typically has a higher interest rate. **($$)**

secondary offering When stock is sold by existing shareholders. An additional stock offering by a company is a follow-on offering.

Secretary of State's Office A state agency that registers a variety of business organizations, including corporations, assumed business names, banks, insurance companies, limited liability companies, limited liability partnerships and limited partnerships. Other business-related filings include trade and service marks, auctioneer's licenses and legal newspaper registrations, among others.

sector An industry within the economy where the companies all sell the same product or service.

sector fund A mutual fund that invests primarily in companies that are in the same industry. **($$$)**

secured creditor People or companies owed debt that is backed by collateral, such as a car loan or a home mortgage. **($$$)**

Securities and Exchange Commission The regulatory agency that oversees all publicly traded companies and investing. The SEC requires all public and some private companies to file documents regularly so investors can gauge the performance of the business. In addition, the SEC protects investors from manipulation and fraud by requiring the registration of securities sold by wire or on the Internet. *SEC* is acceptable on second reference.

securitization The process where an issuer packages a group of assets and markets the package to investors. Mortgage-backed securities sold to investors are an example of an asset that has gone through the securitization process. **($$$$)**

Seeing Eye dog A trademarked product. There is no hyphen. The generic term is guide dog.

sell A rating given a stock by a sell-side analyst. A "sell" rating is the lowest rating an analyst can give. There are generally far fewer "sell" ratings than "buy" ratings.

sell-side analyst Used to describe the retail brokers and research departments that sell securities and make recommendations for the brokerage firm's customers. Do not use interchangeably with **buy-side analyst.**

selling, general and administrative expense An expense incurred by a company to operate. Such expenses include marketing and advertising costs, salaries, telephone bills, electricity and heating, and rent. The term is a line on a company's income statement. *SG&A* is acceptable on second reference.

sell-off (n.), sell off (v.) The fast selling of a stock, bond or commodity, which causes the price of the equity to decline.

senior debt A bond or other form of debt that has precedence over other debt issued by the same issuer. If the entity files for bankruptcy protection, the senior debt is repaid first. It can also be called a *senior security*. **($$$$)**

shareholder An investor who owns at least one share of a company. Can also be called a *stockholder*. Shareholders are some of the most important sources when following a company. Go to annual meetings and hand your business card to them, and call them regularly to ask them about events going on at the company.

shareholder activist An investor who uses his or her position as a shareholder in a company to attempt to force a change at the business. Shareholder activists will submit proposals to be included in the company's proxy statement and to be voted on at the annual meeting. They are often about issues such as the company's business in developing countries and how workers in those areas are treated. A shareholder activist, often a euphemism for **corporate raider,** is not the same as a **gadfly.** Do not use the terms interchangeably.

shareholder equity A firm's total assets minus total liabilities. Also known as *capital* or *net worth.* **($$)**

shareholder rights plan A written document that outlines the rights of shareholders in a corporation. In most cases, the plan includes provisions that allow a company's board of directors to act on behalf of the shareholders to prevent a **hostile takeover.** A *poison pill* is a type of shareholder rights plan. **($$$$$)**

shareholder value The value that shareholders of a company receive by management's ability to increase earnings, the stock price and dividends. "Increasing shareholder value" is often a euphemism for "getting the stock price up."

share repurchase plan A company's plan to buy back its own shares, reducing the number of outstanding shares. Also referred to as a *buyback plan.* **($$)**

Sheetrock A trademarked product. The generic term is gypsum wallboard.

shelf registration A Securities and Exchange Commission regulation that allows a company to file documents to sell shares but wait up to three years before actually executing its stock offering, i.e. keeping it "on the shelf." The regulation allows companies to avoid bad market conditions and take advantage of favorable investment trends. The documents can be referred to as a *shelf filing.* **($$$$)**

Sherwin-Williams Co. The Cleveland-based paint company's name is hyphenated.

short interest The percentage of shares in a company that are held by investors shorting the stock divided by the number of outstanding shares. A company with a large short interest may indicate negative investor sentiment about the company. **($$$$$)**

short selling The selling of a security that the seller does not own but has borrowed, or any sale that is completed by the delivery of a security borrowed by the seller. Short selling is a legitimate trading strategy. Short sellers bet that they will be able to buy the stock at a lower price than the price at which they sold short.

Short sellers generally employ this strategy if they believe there is a disconnect between the share price and the underlying fundamentals. However, it is also part of various hedging strategies and stock arbitrage. Can also be referred to as *shorting* a stock. The percentage of stock in a company that has been borrowed by short sellers is called the *short interest*. See **naked shorting. ($$$$$)**

short squeeze A situation in which a lack of supply and an increase in demand force a stock price to rise. A short squeeze can be a strategy encouraged by a company, or forced by long investors, to reduce a short position in a stock. It hurts investors who are shorting the stock, forcing them to cover their short positions at substantial losses. **($$$$$)**

short term Bonds that mature in less than one year, or liabilities that are due in less than one year. Specify the time period in a story.

shortfall Amount by which a financial objective has not been met.

sick building syndrome When a building's ventilation or air-conditioning systems are flawed, causing workers to become ill with a number of maladies.

skin in the game A term used to describe when executives use their own money to purchase stock in the company they're operating, or a fund

manager puts his or her own money into the fund, or a company that owns stakes in assets it has securitized. **($$$)**

skirt length theory The humorous idea that skirt lengths are an indicator of the stock market's direction. If skirts are becoming shorter, then the market is supposed to rise, and vice versa. **($$$$)**

small cap A stock with a market capitalization between $300 million and $2 billion.

small business A business that is typically privately owned and a has a few employees. The legal definition is a business with fewer than 100 employees in the United States and fewer than 50 employees in the European Union. A small business needs to have at least 10 employees for the term to be used. Otherwise, it's a **microbusiness.**

Small Business Administration A federal government agency that provides support to small businesses in the form of loans or loan guarantees. *SBA* is acceptable on second reference.

small business investment company A private company that is licensed by the Small Business Administration and makes investments in small businesses, generally at more favorable terms than **venture capital** funds.

SmartMoney A monthly personal finance magazine started in 1992 as a joint venture between Dow Jones & Co. and Hearst Corp. The M is capitalized in the name although it's spelled as one word.

Social Security Administration A federal government agency designed to provide disability, retirement and survivor benefits. It was founded in 1935 and has been funded by taxes taken out of employee paychecks and from employers. The administration is located in Woodland, Md., not in Washington, D.C. Avoid *SSA* on all references.

soft goods Goods that may only be used once or have a lifespan of less than three years. Examples are cosmetics, fuel, food and clothing. Also called *nondurable goods.* **($$$)**

sole proprietorship An unincorporated business that is owned by one person who pays personal income taxes on any profit the business makes.

sourcing A hot issue in business journalism. In some ways, sourcing of information when writing about business is easier than in other fields because there are plenty of government documents, such as Securities and Exchange Commission filings. But in other ways, sourcing for stories can be extremely complicated, particularly when using sources such as company employees whose jobs could be lost if their superiors knew they were talking to a journalist. In addition, sources in the business world always have an agenda — whether it's to make their company look better or worse in the public eye, or to make money in the markets.

Here are some general rules that should be applied when sourcing business news stories:

1. Limit off-the-record sourcing as much as possible. If a source tells you something off the record, verify the information from another source or two before feeling comfortable using it.

2. Use caution with sources who don't want information attributed to themselves. Such sources would like a journalist to publicize the information, but don't want their name attached to it. Ask yourself why that's the case.

3. Back up what people say as much as possible with information contained in documents.

4. Avoid using company spokesmen and spokeswomen whenever possible. A manager or executive of the company should be the ones speaking for the company, particularly when the questions involve its day-to-day operations.

5. That said, realize that PR people within companies can be valuable sources of information and willing to provide excellent fact nuggets if you gain their trust as a responsible business journalist.

6. Feel free to use internal company documents as sources of information. Cultivate sources willing to provide such information.

7. Disclose potential conflicts for on-the-record sources in your stories during the first attribution. Explain that the hedge fund manager quoted about a company's poor management is shorting the stock, or that the sell-side analyst works for a firm that performs investment banking for the company.

8. Avoid using the same sources over and over again about the same topic or when writing about the same company. Find new sources to use. Long-time readers will recognize that you're going back to the same quote hounds and get turned off.

9. Realize that virtually everyone you encounter while reporting a story has a potential conflict. Independent industry consultants may want to curry favor with a company. Business school professors may want a spot on the company's board.

10. Always verify the source of information, particularly information from the Internet. Bloomberg News has a policy of attributing breaking news to the company's press release and how the release was distributed, such as via PR Newswire or Business Wire, if it is unable to verify the release with the company before publishing the first story. This policy is based on a hoax where a story was written based on a fake release.

solvent A situation in which a company's assets exceed its liabilities. The antonym is **insolvent.**

Spam A trademarked product. The generic term is luncheon meat. Lowercase, *spam* is acceptable for unsolicited e-mail.

specialist An exchange member who buys and sells a particular stock, holding inventory to trade with investors. There is at least one specialist in every major stock traded. **($$$$)**

speculator An investor who takes large risks, hoping for a return that vastly exceeds the norms of a market. Speculators often invest in sophisticated equities such as futures and options or in shorting stock.

spinoff (n.) A subsidiary or a division of one company that becomes its own separate company. Spinoff companies are intended to be worth more separately than they were as a subsidiary of a larger company. The verb is **spin off.**

split-adjusted price A stock price that reflects historical stock splits. For example, a stock that was worth $10 in 2000 has since undergone two 2-for-1 stock splits, and the stock price is currently trading at $15. While the price may have appeared to have gone up 50 percent, it's actually risen more than that. The 2000 stock price, on a *split-adjusted* basis, is actually $2.50 **($$$$$)**

spokesman, spokeswoman Acceptable terms when referring to company public relations personnel. *Representative* is an acceptable gender-neutral substitute. The term also can be applied to a celebrity who appears in advertising to endorse a product.

spot market The commodities market in which goods are sold for cash and delivered immediately. It's also called the *cash market*. **($$$)**

spread The difference between the **bid** and **ask** prices of a security.

squawk box An intercom speaker on the desks of brokers that allows them to hear sell-side analysts at the firm's research department discuss stocks. When used as the name of the CNBC show, it should be capitalized and places in quotation marks. **($$$)**

squeeze Used to describe a time period when lending is difficult, or when higher costs cannot be passed on to customers. During such a time, profits are said to be *squeezed*. **($$)**

stake A term used to describe how much an investor owns in a company.

Standard & Poor's Corp. A New York-based company that rates stocks and bonds. Its parent is McGraw-Hill Cos.

standard of living A level of wealth, ownership of material goods and income required to obtain a specific so-cioeconomic standing in a community. The standard of living fluctuates depending on a community. A high standard of living in Atlanta is less expensive than an equivalent high standard of living in New York.

standstill agreement Can refer to a contract that stops a **hostile takeover,** or to when a lender stops demanding the payment of a loan from a borrower and new loan terms are then negotiated. **($$$$$)**

startup A new company, sometimes one without any revenue. **Start up** is the verb.

Steak n Shake Co. The Indianapolis-based restaurant chain uses no apostrophes in its name, even though its logo appears to use one.

stock Ownership in a company that is represented by shares. A holder of stock (a shareholder) has a claim on a part of its assets and earnings. Also known as an **equity.**

stock index A method of measuring the performance of the stock market. Indexes will also measure the performance of stocks in certain industries or countries. Do **not** call the Dow Jones industrial average a stock index. It is an average. Indexes are price-weighted.

stock market stories Too often reporters overplay or underplay a daily change in the stock market by how it is described. The following guidelines should be applied when using verbs to describe how a broad market index has fluctuated:

1 percent drop or less: Use "fell" or "dropped," as well as "declined." And we're even OK with "moved downward."

2 to 4 percent decline: Any of the above, as well as "dipped" and "slumped," which are slightly more serious grades of a fall.

5 to 10 percent decline: "sell-off" is appropriate here, as is "retreated." On Wednesday, Oct. 15, 2008, the market "retreated" by 7.87 percent.

Drop of 10 percent or more: The term "rout" is correct. The stock market fell by 12.8 percent on Oct. 28, 1929, the first day of the decline that preceded the Great Depression. "Rout" needs to convey the suddenness of the move. On Oct. 19, 1987, the market was "routed" when the Dow Jones Industrial Average fell 22.6 percent that day.

Multi-day drops that total more than 10 percent would also equal a "rout" as long as it's clear that the term refers to more than one day. Do **not** use "correction" in any instance. It is a euphemism.

Here are the verbs recommended when writing about increases:

Rise of up to 1 percent: "Increased" and "advanced" are the most common accepted terms. "Gained" is good as well.

2 to 4 percent increase: Again, "gained," "increased" or "advanced" is fine here, as are "rose" and "grew."

5 to 10 percent increase: "Jumped" and "soared" are appropriate here.

10 percent or more: "Surged" is the best antonym for "was routed." When the Dow rose by 936 points on Oct. 13, 2008, it surged by 11 percent, the fifth-largest one-day percentage gain in the market's history. The market has only had six one-day surges in its history.

stock options The opportunity, given by your employer, to purchase a certain number of shares of your company's common stock at a pre-established price, known as the exercise price, during a specific period of time. The options mature during various periods, known as *vesting periods*. **($$$)**

stock split Increase in a corporation's number of outstanding shares of stock without any change in the shareholders' equity or the aggregate market value at the time of the split. In a split, the share price declines. In a reverse split, the stock price rises. Begin with the number of shares an investor will have after the split. **($$)**

stock symbol A series of letters that an exchange assigns to represent the stock of a specific company. For example, Coca-Cola Co.'s stock symbol is KO. No two stock symbols are alike. Also called a *stock ticker* or a *ticker symbol*. Avoid using a stock symbol in a story to refer to a company.

stockbroker A person who executes buy and sell orders on securities in return for a fee or a commission. Not to be confused with a **financial planner** or **financial adviser.**

stockholder A person who owns at least one share of stock in a company. Also called a *shareholder.*

stop order An order to buy or sell a stock when the price passes a particular point. It allows investors to lock in profits or limit their losses. Also called a *stop-loss order.* **($$$)**

straddle An options strategy in which the investor holds a **call** and a **put** option for the same security. It's an investment strategy that some investors use when they believe the price of a stock will move, but are unsure which way. **($$$$$)**

strategic alternatives A term used by a company when it announces a review of its operations, which may include a sale of some or all of its operations. It's often a euphemism for a company putting itself up for sale.

TheStreet.com A Wall Street-focused financial news site co-founded in 1996 by Jim Cramer. When writing the name, capitalize the S and use the .com.

street name When securities are held in the name of the broker instead of the specific investor. Such a move makes it easier to transfer the stock to another investor if it is sold.

strike price The price at which a derivatives contract, such as a call option, can be exercised. Also known as the *exercise price.* **($$$)**

structured finance Highly complex financial transactions such as a **collateralized debt obligation** or a **collateralized mortgage obligation.** **($$$$$)**

Styrofoam A trademarked product used mainly for insulation. The generic term is foam plastic. There is no such thing as a Styrofoam cup.

subordinated debt A bond or other debenture that ranks behind **senior debt** in terms of being repaid. Also called *subordinated security.* **($$$)**

sub-prime mortgage A loan with a higher-than-average interest rate offered to a consumer who presumably cannot qualify for a loan at the normal rate because of credit ratings or other problems. **($$)**

subsidiary A company where more than 50 percent of the voting stock is controlled by another company.

Super Bowl indicator An indicator based on the belief that when a team from the old National Football League wins the Super Bowl, the stock market will rise in the coming year; conversely, when a team from the old American Football League wins the Super Bowl, the stock market will fall in the coming year. It is not meant to be taken seriously. **($$$$$)**

Supervalu Inc. Lowercase the name of the Eden Prairie, Minn.-based grocery store chain after the S.

surplus A situation in which exports exceed imports or assets exceed liabilities.

suspended trading The stoppage of trading in a security, primarily due to a lack of material important information. A stock can be suspended because a company has failed to file recent financial information with the Securities and Exchange Commission. **($$$)**

swap The exchange of one security for another. A swap can also occur with currencies and with interest rates. Explain what is being swapped in the story.

sweetheart deal An offer or agreement that is so advantageous to one party that it is difficult to turn down. It can be an acquisition offer, a compensation package or any other type of business deal.

syndicate A group that works together on a large project, such as a corporate loan. **($$$)**

synergy Used mostly in the context of mergers and acquisitions, synergy is the idea — often erroneous — that the value and performance of two companies combined will be greater than the sum of the separate parts.

Sysco Corp. Lowercase all but the first letter of the Houston-based food supplier's name.

Tabasco A trademarked product. The generic term is hot-pepper sauce.

takeover Change in controlling interest of a corporation. A takeover may be a friendly acquisition or an unfriendly bid that the target company may fight. If the company is publicly traded, then the acquiring company will make an offer for the outstanding shares. **Take over** is the verb.

takeover artist An investor who tries to find companies that are attractive to purchase and that can be turned around and sold for a profit. Carl Icahn is an example of a takeover artist.

tangible net worth A measure of the worth of the physical assets of a company, excluding intangible assets such as **goodwill,** patents and brand names. **($$$)**

TARP The Troubled Asset Relief Program originally created by the federal government in 2008 to purchase troubled assets from financial companies to improve their finances, but later used to provide capital to banks and to companies such as GM and American International Group Inc. **($$$$)**

tax-free bond A bond issued by a municipal, county or state government where the interest payments are not taxable by the federal government. Also called *tax-exempt bonds.* **($$)**

taxable income The amount of income by an individual or a company that's taxable by the federal, state or local government.

TD Ameritrade Holding Corp. Capitalize only the first letter in Ameritrade, in contrast to the all capitalization used by the Omaha, Neb.-based broker. Use *TD Ameritrade* on second reference.

technical analysis A method of evaluating an equity by looking at data such as historical prices and volume traded. **($$$)**

technology terms The growing use of technology in all forms of business, and the increasing importance of the technology industry itself, has resulted in many technology-related words, phrases, acronyms and abbreviations entering the language. Still, many people are unfamiliar with much of this terminology. When writing about technology or mentioning technology, we recommend explaining as much as possible. If you think a word or term might be unfamiliar to any of your readers or viewers, then explain or define it

Here are some technology terms that seem common in everyday language but may still cause confusion. If you don't know what all of these terms mean, then it's a good indication that even basic technology words and phrases need to be explained in business writing.

application: A software program loaded into a smartphone such as a Droid, a social networking site such as Facebook or tablet such as an iPad. *App* or *apps* is acceptable on second reference. **($$$)**

back-end: A database that is accessed by a user through an external application.

back up (v.): To copy files or directories onto a separate storage device to protect it from being lost in case of a computer drive failure.

bitmap: A type of memory used to store digital images.

Blu-ray: A disc storage format for data and high-definition video storage.

broadband: An Internet connection that allows for faster interaction than dial-up access.

browser: A software program such as Internet Explorer or Mozilla Firefox that allows you to search the Internet for information.

cookie: Data sent to a website each time the site is accessed so that the site identifies the specific user.

CPM: Stands for cost per mille. It's a uniform rate for Internet advertising that specifies a rate to be paid for every thousand page views.

domain name: An Internet website address. http://www.chrisroush. com is the domain name of one of the authors of this stylebook.

download: The transfer of data from a server or the Internet to a personal computer hard drive.

DPI: Stands for dots per inch. It measures the resolution of a photo or a scanner.

end user: The person or persons who actually use the software or website.

firmware: The programs that control an electronic device.

front-end: The application that allows a user to access a database.

flash drive: A portable storage device that plugs into a computer's USB port.

HTML: Stands for Hypertext Markup Language. It is programming language used to create documents for display on the Internet.

hyperlink: A connection between websites. It can also be called a *link*.

Intranet: A private, internal Internet connection for an organization or company.

ISP: Stands for Internet Service Provider. An example is AOL.

Javascript: A trademarked product. The generic term is scripting software. It's a programming language primarily used to build websites.

JPEG: Stands for Joint Photographic Experts Group. It is a compressed graphics format for photos and graphics.

LCD: Stands for liquid crystal display. It is a flat, electronic display that does not emit light directly and is used in video games, computer monitors, watches and televisions.

LED: Stands for light-emitting diode. They are used as indicator lights in many devices, such as telling the user whether the device is on or off as well as for aviation, signage and street lighting. LEDs are increasingly being used in household lighting.

memory: The amount of computer data storage available.

MPEG: Stands for Moving Pictures Experts Group. It is the name of an audio/video file format.

MP3: A common format for storing audio such as songs on digital audio players.

MP4: A method of storing audio and video content.

open source: Software where the coding is provided to the users under a licensing agreement, allowing users to make modifications to fit their needs.

operating system: A program that allows software to run on a computer or another consumer electronics item such as a mobile phone or GPS device. Unix and Microsoft Windows are examples.

page views: The number of downloads for a website, even if it is from the same user. One person who visits the same website 500 times in one day, or who visits 500 different pages within one domain, will register as 500 page views but only one unique visitor for that day.

PDF: Stands for Portable Document Format. Created by Adobe Systems, it allows computer users to view documents through its universal format. **($$)**

peripheral: A piece of computer hardware added to a computer to expand its capabilities, such as a scanner or a printer.

pixel: One dot on a computer screen or one dot in an image from a digital camera. Short for PICture ELement. The resolution of a photograph or computer is stated in pixels per inch, or PPI. The size of an image is stated in megapixels, or 1million pixels. It is determined by multiplying the width of an image in pixels times its depth in pixels. A camera with a 14-megapixel sensor can produce a larger-size sharp photographic print than can an 8-megapixel camera. In printing, pixels per inch roughly translate into dots per inch. **($$$)**

plasma: A type of flat-panel display commonly used with large televisions. Plasma displays are not to be confused with LCDs.

rich text: Text that has been enhanced with formatting or multimedia. E-mail messages with graphics are considered rich text.

RSS: Stands for Really Simple Syndication, which allows material from the Web to be published in a standardized format.

smartphone: A hand-held computer device that has many of the same functions as a PC but also operates as a telephone. Sometimes known as a *personal digital assistant*, or *PDA*.

source code: The underlying code that makes up a software program.

streaming: The transmission of digital audio or video on a website.

URL: Stands for Uniform Resource Locator. It's the address of a site on the Internet.

USB: Stands for Universal Serial Bus. It is the most common type of connector that allows consumers to download photos, documents and other files onto a computer.

VOIP: Stands for Voice Over Internet Protocol. It allows people to transmit their voices and talk to each other using the Internet with services such as Skype.

Web 2.0: Used to describe a new generation on the Internet where pages are no longer static and content can be entered or manipulated on sites.

Wi-Fi: A trademark of the Wi-Fi Alliance, so it is always capitalized. The term is used to describe gadgets that can access wireless local area networks.

tender As a verb, to make or accept a formal offer, such as a takeover. It can also be a noun meaning a bid to purchase Treasury securities.

tender offer An offer to shareholders to purchase some or all or their shares. The price offered is usually at a premium to the market price. Tender offers may be friendly or unfriendly. **($$$)**

term life insurance A policy with a specific duration, such as 10 years. When the policy term ends, the policyholder must decide whether to renew for another term, often at a higher premium. Term insurance carries no cash value.

thrift A financial institution that focuses on deposits and making mortgage loans in the local community. It can also be called a **savings and loan** or a savings bank.

3M Co. The St. Paul-Minn.-based company's name uses the numeral 3 and the capital M in all references.

TIAA-CREF Stands for Teachers Insurance and Annuity Association — College Retirement Equities Fund. It's a nonprofit organization that manages retirement funds for employees in the education, medicine and research fields. *TIAA-CREF* is acceptable on all references.

ticker tape A computerized device that delivers market information — the ticker symbol, amount of shares traded and latest price of a stock — to investors around the world. The term "ticker" comes from a telegraph machine invented in 1867 to distribute stock prices that was later updated by Thomas Edison, who fixed the Gold Indicator Co.'s telegraph that relayed gold prices to customers. (**$**)

title insurance A policy purchased by home buyers that protects the lender from pre-existing liens against the property. (**$**)

titles Capitalize all business titles when used before a person's name. **CEO** is acceptable on first reference. Other title abbreviations, such as **CFO**, **COO** and **CIO**, are acceptable on second reference. Lower case and spell out titles when they stand alone or after a person's name. Occupational titles should be lower case in all references. Although a company may capitalize a title, follow these rules.

TiVo A trademarked product. The generic term is digital TV recorder.

tombstone An advertisement by an investment banker of the offering of a security that gives details such as how many shares were sold and who other underwriters are. A tombstone can also be run by an investment banker that provides services for a merger or acquisition. (**$$$**)

too big to fail A concept in current U.S. economic policy that the largest companies are so interconnected that the government cannot allow them to go under because the financial system and the economy would go into a downward spiral. An example of a company deemed "too big to fail" is the insurer American International Group Inc.

toxic assets Financial assets whose values have dropped dramatically and no longer attract much interest from investors. A slang term, it's generally used to refer to **collateralized debt obligations** and **credit default swaps**. (**$$$$**)

Toys R Us Inc. There is no need for the apostrophes around the R in the Wayne, N.J.-based retailer's name.

tracking stock Stock issued by a parent company that rises or falls based on the performance of a specific division, not the entire company.

trade The buying or selling of a security, such as a stock or bond. Also, the buying and selling of goods and services between economies. Trade statistics are measures taken by the Census Bureau and released six weeks after the end of a month. The story focuses on the change in the overall balance of trade as well as total imports and total exports.

trade deficit When the buying and selling of goods and services result in a country importing goods worth more than what it exports.

trade surplus When exports exceed imports. The United States has not had a trade surplus for an entire year since 1975.

trademark names Use the generic equivalent unless the trademark name is essential to the story. Never use a trademark as a thing; for example, it's Scotch-brand adhesive tape, not Scotch Tape.

trading floor Where equities are traded. Trading can occur at an exchange or at a brokerage house or investment bank. The area is also called *the pit.*

transfer agent A financial institution that keeps a record of all investors and their account balances in a company. Some companies will act as their own transfer agent. **($$$$)**

transumer It has at least two meanings: 1. A consumer who tends to rent, rather than buy, consumer goods. Transumers may rent cars from Zipcar and even rent such items as high-fashion handbags. 2. A consumer who tends to shop heavily in transit, for example, while waiting for a plane connection. **($$$)**

Treasury bill Short-term debt issued by the federal government that has a maturity of less than one year. Bills are sold in $1,000 denominations. The term *T-bill* is also acceptable.

Treasury bond Debt issued by the federal government that has a maturity of more than 10 years. It can also be referred to as a *T-bond* on second reference.

Treasury Department The federal government agency responsible for the issuing of Treasury bonds, notes and bills. The U.S. Mint, however, prints money.

Treasury Inflation Protected Securities A special type of Treasury note or bond that offers protection against inflation. TIPS pay interest on a principal amount that rises or falls based on the consumer price index. *TIPS* is acceptable on second reference. **($$$$$)**

Treasury note Debt issued by the federal government that has a maturity between one year and 10 years. It can be referred to as a *T-note* on second reference.

Treasury securities The term covers Treasury bills, bonds and notes and

Treasury Inflation-Protected Securities. Together, they may be referred to as *Treasurys*.

trend analysis A segment of technical analysis that attempts to predict the future price of a stock based on past data. **($$$)**

triple net lease A lease agreement in which the tenant is responsible for costs associated with the building, such as property taxes, insurance and the cost of repairs and maintenance. The rent payment is generally lower for such leases. **($$$$$)**

triple witching The date when contracts expire for stock index futures, stock index options and stock options. It occurs four times a year, on the third Friday of March, June, September and December. It can be referred to as *freaky Friday* after it's been explained. **($$$$$)**

trustee A court-appointed representative who administers a business or estate. Can be assigned if creditors or others argue that the company is unfit to manage its operations. **($)**

tuck-in acquisition A deal made by a company where the acquired business is folded into an existing division, often to expand its product line or geographic territory. It can also be called a *bolt-on acquisition*. **($$)**

turnaround A situation where a company that has struggled in the past has turned around and improved its operations dramatically. Explain how the turnaround has occurred in a story.

turnover The number of times an asset is replaced during a financial period. A retailer wants a high turnover number because it means that its inventory is not sitting on shelves. It can also be called the *turn*. **($$)**

UAL Corp. The parent company of United Airlines, based in Chicago. *UAL* is acceptable on second reference.

underperform A rating given a stock by a sell-side analyst. An "underperform" rating is slightly better than a "sell" rating, but not as good as a "neutral" rating.

undervalued A stock that is trading below its perceived value. The opposite is **overvalued**. **($$)**

underwater options Stock options where the exercise price is higher than the current price on the market. **($$$)**

underwriter The Wall Street firm that works with a company to sell its shares to the investment world. The underwriter helps determine a price for the stock, then acquires the stock and sells it to investors, who are often its clients. An underwriter receives a fee from the company selling the stock for its services and also receives commissions when selling the stock. **($)**

underwriter discount The difference between the price the lead underwriter pays for the initial public offering shares and the price it resells those shares to other members of the syndicate. **($$$$)**

unemployment rate A measure of how many people are out of the labor force but are looking for work. Measured by the Bureau of Labor Statistics, the monthly data comes out the first Friday of the following month. When writing about unemployment, reporters can write about the unemployment rate, which is the total number of people out of work but looking for work divided by the total workforce. They may also write about the change in the total number of people working, which in some cases might be the more relevant number. For example, the unemployment rate can decline in a month where the total number of people working also declines if the number of discouraged workers — those who have stopped looking for work — increases. **($$)**

Uniform Commercial Code A set of laws regulating commercial transactions, especially those involving the sale of goods where money is borrowed. A UCC filing is a document submitted to the state Secretary of State's Office indicating that the filer has a claim against an asset. UCC is acceptable on second reference to the code.

union An organization of workers who have joined together to benefit the entire group.

union shop An employer that requires new workers to join the union within a certain time period.

UnitedHealth Group Inc. The Minnetonka, Minn., parent company of UnitedHealthcare, one of the largest health insurers in the country.

unlisted stock A stock that trades via a dealer network instead of through an exchange. It's also called an **over-the-counter stock**. These stocks don't trade on exchanges because they're often too small to meet the exchange requirements. In addition, such stocks often are considered volatile. **($$$)**

unrealized gain/loss A potential profit or loss from holding an asset. The opposite is **realized gain/loss.**

unsecured creditors People or companies owed debt that is not backed by collateral. **($$$)**

upgrade The act of a sell-side analyst raising his or her rating on a stock. An upgrade could be from a "neutral" rating to an "outperform" rating, for example.

UPS Acceptable in all references for Atlanta-based United Parcel Service Inc.

uptick An investment transaction occurring above the previous price. When a stock is purchased for $15 a share in one transaction, and then $15.10 in the next transaction, this is considered an uptick. **($$)**

upside-down mortgage A mortgage where the amount owed on the mortgage is more than the value of the home. This occurs in slumping real estate markets. **($$$)**

US Airways Group Inc. No periods are used in the name of the parent company of US Airways.

USAA The San Antonio, Texas-based insurer that sells policies only to military members and their families. Use all caps.

U.S. Green Building Council The nonprofit trade organization behind LEED certification. Try to avoid USGBC, referring instead to the organization. It is based in Washington, D.C. **($$$$)**

U.S. Tax Court A special federal court that decides issues of taxation, such as litigation involving federal income taxes not paid. A company charged with failing to pay enough taxes to the government could go to U.S. Tax Court to resolve the dispute. *Tax court* is acceptable on second reference.

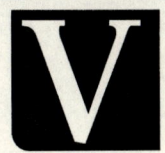

value fund A mutual fund that invests in stocks that are considered to be undervalued in price and often pay dividends. **($$$)**

value, worth Although often used interchangeably, these words have different meanings. The worth of something is its relative merit or importance to an individual or organization. The value of something is how much it can be exchanged for in currency. A share of Coca-Cola stock can be *valued* at $45 a share but its *worth* to an investor could be more than the *value* because the investor is a descendant of the family that founded the company.

variable annuity An insurance contract in which the insurance company guarantees a minimum payment, but actual payments depend on returns of the assets in which the premiums are invested. Variable annuities were popular purchases in the 1990s when the stock market rose, but have since fallen out of favor. **($$)**

Vaseline A trademarked product. The generic term is petroleum jelly.

Velcro A trademarked product. The generic term is fabric fastener.

venture capital Funds made available to start-up companies and small businesses, typically in return for an ownership stake and a say in how the operation is managed. A venture capital firm invests money in such companies, expecting that the company receiving the funds will grow and become successful. **($)**

versus Abbreviate as v. when writing about lawsuits.

vest To convey to a person a legal authority or possession. When **restricted stock** *vests*, it becomes the property of the employee. **($$)**

vested interest A financial or personal stake in an operation. An investor in a company may take over as chief executive officer in an attempt to improve its operations because he or she has a *vested interest* in improving its performance.

vice chairman A title given to a member of the board of directors who is second in command to the chairman. In reality, the vice chairman title is often given to executives who have lost out in a bid to become the chief executive officer of a company.

vice president A title of a company executive. Capitalize when used before the name. Do not use VP.

VF Corp. The Greensboro, N.C.-based company is the world's largest maker of blue jeans, including the Lee, Wrangler and Rustler brands. It uses no periods in its name.

Visa Inc. Lowercase all but the first letter in the name of the credit card company, based in Foster City, Calif.

volume The number of units traded in a market or exchange during a certain point of time, such as a day or a week. An increase or decrease in volume may indicate investor sentiment has changed.

vulture fund A fund that buys distressed securities, such as the bonds of companies that have filed for bankruptcy court protection or junk bonds of companies that are likely to default on its interest payments. **($$$$)**

Wal-Mart Stores Inc. *Wal-Mart* is acceptable on second reference for the world's largest retailer, with headquarters in Bentonville, Ark. Though the company logo no longer contains a hyphen, the official company name does. Refer, however, to the stores as *Walmart stores.*

Wall Street A term used to describe the financial and investment community in the United States. It comes from the original location of the New York Stock Exchange in lower Manhattan. The term can also be used in writing to refer to the overall stock market, as in *Wall Street fell Monday in heavy trading amid concerns about inflation and a drop in consumer spending.* In such cases, *the Street* is acceptable. A variant meaning is a large financial institution.

The Wall Street Journal A daily U.S. business newspaper founded in 1889, The Wall Street Journal is considered the leading source of business news in the United States. In 2007, its parent company, Dow Jones & Co., was sold to News Corp., leading some to question whether the paper's coverage would remain independent under Rupert Murdoch's ownership. *The* is always capitalized when used as part of the paper's name. The abbreviation *WSJ* is acceptable in headlines only. On second reference, use *The Journal.*

warehouse lender A short-term lender for mortgage banks. **($$$$)**

warrant A derivative security that gives the holder the right to purchase securities from the issuer at a certain price and a certain time. The difference between a warrant and a **call option** is that a warrant is issued by the company. **($$$$$)**

WARN Act The Worker Adjustment and Retraining Notification Act. It was enacted in August 1988 and became effective February 1989. This law requires companies with 100 or more workers to give a state labor department or similar agency 60 days' notice when laying off employees. A WARN Act notice is a public record. *WARN Act* is acceptable in all references.

Washington Mutual Inc. *WaMu* is acceptable on second reference to the Seattle-based bank, closed by regulators in 2008, now part of JPMorgan Chase.

weather derivative A financial instrument used by a company to hedge against the possibility of weather-related losses, such as attendance at an outdoor concert being reduced by rain. If the losses do not occur, then the investor who purchases the instrument makes a profit. If the losses do occur, then the company receives payment from the investor. **($$$$$)**

WebMD Health Corp. Capitalize the MD when referring to the New York-based online medical information provider.

WellPoint Inc. The name of the Indianapolis-based health insurance company is one word.

when-issued (adj.), when issued (v.) A transaction that is agreed upon before a stock actually begins trading. Stock splits and new issues are traded on a *when-issued basis.*

whisper number An unofficial earnings per share estimate for a company that circulates on Wall Street before a company actually releases its earnings. The whisper number may be very different from the published earnings-per-share estimate from **sell-side analysts**, and it's sometimes given to favored investors. **($$$)**

whistle-blower An employee who thinks he or she has knowledge of illegal activity within a company and "blows the whistle" by providing that information to a regulatory agency or media outlet.

white collar A description of an employee who does no manual labor. Many Wall Street workers are *white-collar employees.*

white knight A company that makes a **friendly takeover** offer to another company that is the subject of a **hostile takeover**.

white-shoe firm A slang term for an old-line, broker-dealer organization or law firm. The term should be explained in almost all references. **($$$$$)**

whole life insurance A policy with both insurance and investment parts that pays a guaranteed amount upon the death of the policyholder and has a cash value.

WH Smith PLC The name of the British-based bookstore chain uses no periods.

Wieden & Kennedy Use an ampersand, not a plus sign, in the name of the Portland, Ore.-based advertising agency.

Windbreaker A trademarked product. The generic term is lightweight jacket.

Windex A trademarked product. The generic term is glass cleaner.

widow-and-orphan stock A low-risk stock that pays dividends, such as utilities stocks. They are considered some of the safest stocks in the market, although they are not without risk. General Motors Corp. was once considered a widow-and-orphan stock, as were bank stocks. **($$$)**

wire house A company whose offices are connected by communications systems that allow any piece of financial information or prices for financial products to be transmitted back and forth. A bank is considered a wire house, though the term bank is preferred. **($$$)**

Wired A technology-oriented business magazine acquired by Conde Nast Publications in 1998 and founded in 1993.

Wite-Out A trademarked product. Note the hyphen and capital O. The generic term is correction fluid.

workers' compensation Insurance purchased by companies that pays benefits to workers when they are injured on the job. This type of insurance is required by state regulators. Note that the apostrophe comes after the s. **($$)**

working capital Current assets minus current liabilities. Working capital is considered a measure of a company's financial health. Positive working capital means a company is able to pay off its short-term debt. **($$)**

WorldCom The company that produced the largest bankruptcy court filing ever when the filing was made in July 2002, primarily due to accounting scandals. (That record has been surpassed by the Lehman Brothers filing in September 2008 as the largest bankruptcy filing in his-

tory.) The company emerged from bankruptcy court protection in 2004 as MCI Inc., which disappeared when it was acquired by Verizon in 2006. Use *WorldCom* only when referring to the pre-bankruptcy company.

World Trade Organization The international body that governs rules of trade between countries. Its goal is to ensure that trade flows freely.

Worth A personal finance magazine launched in 1992 by Fidelity Investments. It was purchased by Sandow Media in 2008 and relaunched in June 2009 aimed at individuals with a net worth of more than $2 million.

wrap An account in which a broker manages an investor's money for a flat quarterly or annual fee. It avoids **churning,** the practice of a broker trading in an investment account to generate commissions. **($$$$$)**

WR Hambrecht & Co. Use an ampersand instead of the plus sign, and no periods, in the name of the San Francisco-based investment bank.

write-down (n., adj.), write down (v.) Reducing the book value of an asset because it is overvalued compared with market values. Also called a *write-off.*

write-off (n., adj.), write off (v.) A reduction in the value of an asset to its actual worth. Write-offs can decrease earnings for a company. For example,

if a company acquired some machin-
ery in the purchase of another company but then discovered that the
machines were outdated and couldn't
be used to manufacture its products,
it would *write off*, or lower, the value
of those assets on its books.

Xerox A trademarked product. The generic term is photocopy.

Yahoo Inc. Do not use the exclamation point in the name of the company.

year-over-year A comparison that measures the financial performance during the same time period. A company may state that its first-quarter earnings have risen on a *year-over-year* basis for the past five years. That means that its earnings for the first three months of 2009 have been higher than the earnings for the first three months of 2008, which reported earnings slightly higher than the first quarter of 2007, when first-quarter earnings were higher than 2006's first-quarter earnings, which were higher than first-quarter earnings in 2005.

year to date The period beginning Jan. 1 up until the current day. Do not use YTD on any reference.

yield The income return on an investment, divided by its market price. This word can be used to refer to both stocks and bonds.

yield curve A line that plots the interest yields, on a set day, of debt obligations with the same credit rating but different maturity dates. The yield curve is used as a benchmark for other debt. **($$$$)**

yield to maturity The rate of return for a bond if it is held until its maturity date. It can also be referred to simply as the yield. Avoid the abbreviation YTM. **($$$)**

YouTube LLC The name of the San Bruno, Calif., company and its website is one word. It became a division of Google Inc. in 2006.

Yum Brands Inc. Do not use the exclamation point after Yum for the restaurant company based in Louisville, Ky.

Z

zero-coupon bond A bond that doesn't pay any periodic cash interest but is sold for less than its face value and is redeemed at maturity for face value. **($$$$$)**

Ziploc A trademarked product. The generic term is zippered plastic bag.

zoning Government laws that regulate the use of land in an area. In most cases, a company must obtain zoning approval before building.

II. Business news legal issues

I t's not enough for business journalists to know the ins and outs of corporate America and how it works. They also need to know a fair amount of how laws and regulations affect their ability to obtain and use information about companies and individuals in stories.

We cover some of the bigger legal issues involving business journalism in this section. It is by no means complete, but we do believe that it gives a business reporter an overview of what he or she needs to know when confronted with a legal issue.

Annual meetings

In May 2009, the St. Petersburg Times retail reporter was denied access to the annual meeting of the Home Shopping Network. That's not the first time a business journalist has been denied entry into a meeting being held by a company for its shareholders.

In 2006, retailer Target Corp. closed its annual meeting to reporters. In December 2005, New Jersey-based IDT Communications barred a New York Times reporter from attending its annual meeting. In 2001, Yahoo wouldn't allow reporters into its annual meeting, and in 1999, Exxon Mobil wouldn't allow reporters from gay publications into its meeting. In 2001, Pacific Gas & Electric Corp. would not let a reporter from the San Francisco Bay Guardian attend its annual meeting.

No part of federal laws governing publicly traded companies stipulates that the annual shareholders meeting should be open to the public. Shareholders are allowed to attend, but a company can prevent the media from attending.

Many companies, of course, do allow business journalists to attend their annual meetings. Some even provide access to their executives before or after the meeting. But there is no legal provision that states they must do so.

A number of business media outlets have taken the following step to avoid missing out on potential news at an annual meeting — they have bought a share of stock for each company they are interested in covering. With that one share, they can send a reporter to attend the meeting as their representative.

At the 2007 annual meeting of the Society of American Business Editors and Writers, 57 percent of the business journalists in attendance said the practice of a media outlet or a reporter owning shares to attend an annual meeting was acceptable. Another 15 percent said it was acceptable to obtain a proxy statement from a shareholder and use that document to attend the meeting.

Also note that a company holding an annual meeting can make stipulations on journalists attending the meeting. In February 2009, Apple prevented reporters from entering its annual meeting with cellular phones, laptop computers and other communication devices that would have allowed them to blog or report on the meeting as it was happening.

Defamation/privacy

Although defamation and privacy cases often concern themselves with individuals outside the business world, they can also be brought by a company or the executive of a company.

In 2006, real estate developer Donald Trump sued New York Times business journalist Timothy O'Brien, who had written a book about Trump. In his lawsuit, Trump alleged that O'Brien defamed him by stating in the book that his net worth was in the hundreds of millions of dollars, not in the billions of dollars that Trump asserts. A judge ruled in favor of O'Brien and his publisher in 2009 and dismissed the case, stating Trump had not been a victim of actual malice, although Trump vowed to appeal the ruling.

In addition, a number of states have product disparagement or trade libel statutes and also recognize such claims at common law that allow a company to sue business journalists when they have written stories about companies and their products.

Although not a business journalist, talk show host Oprah Winfrey was sued by cattle ranchers in Texas after airing a show in 1996 that called into question what cattle were being fed. The ranchers claimed the show caused a drop in the price of their cattle. A jury ruled in favor of Winfrey.

In the Jan. 13, 1997, edition of Forbes, writer Caroline Waxler wrote in the "Streetwalker" column that shares of Biospherics Inc. were overvalued. The company filed a defamation lawsuit six months later, claiming that its "reputation and business" had been injured. The court denied the company's claims, stating that the column was protected as a statement of opinion. An appeals court affirmed the court's ruling. See the appeal court ruling at: http://lw.bna.com/lw/19980825/981118.htm.

It's important for business journalists to realize that while opinion can be a defense in a defamation action, it does not enjoy blanket protection. Certain elements must be met first, such as disclosing the facts you're basing your opinion on, and not suggesting to your reader that you know other facts you aren't sharing.

HIPAA

Stands for the Health Insurance Portability and Accountability Act, which was enacted in 1996. In 2002, a privacy provision was added that governs the release of health status and coverage information related to individuals.

Essentially, the HIPAA privacy provision prevents the release of medical and health information about individuals to journalists, unless the person signs a waiver of HIPAA. Then, the information can be released to anyone noted in the authorization.

This provision has broad ramifications for business journalists, particularly those who report about the health care or pharmaceutical industries. Often, these reporters seek examples of consumers who suffer from certain illnesses or who are taking specific medications. The reporter cannot obtain information about the consumer's health status from anyone but the patient.

The privacy provision has yet to be tested in terms of other areas, such as what would happen if the health status of the CEO of a company became public interest. For example, in the past few years, the health of Apple CEO Steve Jobs has been a topic of stories for those covering the company. In January 2009, the company released information about Jobs' health when it stated that he would take a leave of absence from his leadership role.

An unanswered question regarding the HIPAA privacy provision remains: What would happen if a business journalist received from an anonymous source the medical records of a company CEO whose health was of great interest to shareholders and wrote an article based on those records? It could be argued that those medical records would be exempt from the privacy provision because of public interest — if the CEO was deathly ill, such news could cause the stock price to drop dramatically. In June 2009, The Wall Street Journal broke the story that Jobs had received a liver transplant at a Tennessee hospital. The story did not attribute the information, but was later confirmed by the hospital.

Insider trading

The connection between illegal insider trading and business journalism has unfortunately been in existence for more than 100 years.

"If a railroad baron wished to manipulate his company stock in the 19th century, he leaked a story to a news agency where it would be circulated at once and trading in the stock affected within an hour or so, bullish or bearish," according to an early history of Dow Jones and The Wall Street Journal. "The baron would pocket the profit, losers be damned."

At The Journal, reporters overseeing the "Broad Street Gossip" and "Abreast of the Market" columns wrote positive stories about specific companies and the stocks in return for money from investors in the 1920s. The revelations about the Journal reporters came out during hearings by the Senate Banking and Currency Committee in 1932, when Congressman Fiorello LaGuardia produced canceled checks written to the Journal reporters. The stories based on the bribes had gone as far back as 1923.

In June 1969, financial columnist Alex Campbell published an item in the Los Angeles Herald Examiner about Amer Systems Inc. Unbeknown to readers, Campbell had purchased 5,000 shares of the company shortly before the article ran. The article, which praised the company, caused the stock to rise. Campbell then sold his stock at a profit. Campbell was charged. A judge who ruled in Campbell's case called his actions "reprehensible." (Campbell and the paper were also sued by two people who sold their company to Amer Systems Inc., arguing that he should have stated his interest in the stock. Read the appeals court ruling in that case at: http://bulk.resource.org/courts.gov/c/F2/594/594. F2d.1261.76-1647.html)

The most famous illegal act involving using the media to profit financially occurred at The Wall Street Journal. In the 1980s, Journal reporter R. Foster Winans was writing the "Heard on the Street" column. He met some stockbrokers and agreed to provide them information about what was going to appear in the column before it was published. The brokers then used that information and made nearly $700,000. They also paid Winans some of their profits.

Winans and the two brokers were convicted of mail and wire fraud charges and for violating securities laws by using confidential information for personal use. A court ruling related to the Winans case, *Carpenter v. United States*, can be found at: http://caselaw.lp.findlaw.com/cgi-bin/getcase. pl$court=US&vol=484&invol=19.

In 1989, Seymour Ruderman, an editor at BusinessWeek, was sentenced to six months in prison for trading on information in the magazine before it was published. He had earned $39,000 in profits with the information. The SEC also brought charges against the editor. The information came from the "Inside Wall Street" column written by Gene Marcial. Ruderman pleaded guilty to two counts of mail fraud. His case can be found at: http://www.sec.gov/news/ digest/1989/dig052689.pdf

And in early 2004, CBS Marketwatch.com commentator Thom Calandra resigned from the online financial journalism site after it was disclosed that the SEC was investigating his trading. The SEC accused him of "scalping," or selling stocks shortly after his positive recommendations about the stocks caused their prices to rise, without disclosing the sales.

Calandra allegedly made more than $400,000 through buying shares of 23 small-cap stocks while writing favorable profiles recommending the stocks, and then selling his shares when the stocks rose after his columns were published. The SEC also accused Calandra of failing to disclose that he was compensated from a stock promoter affiliated with two companies that he profiled.

In 2005, Calandra settled the charges, without admitting or denying the allegations, by paying more than $540,000 in penalties. The complaint against Calandra can be read at: http://www.sec.gov/litigation/complaints/comp19028.pdf

It should be apparent that although the majority of coverage about illegal insider trading in the business media has been about corporate executives, board members and others connected to a company, business journalists are also subject to the insider trading laws. A business journalist cannot use information that he or she gathers in the course of reporting a story to make investments before the story is published and the information is provided to readers or viewers.

Public records

Many federal and state government documents filed by public and private companies are public record by law and can — and should — be used by business journalists in the course of reporting stories.

The most important of these include:

1. Securities and Exchange Commission filings by public and private companies.

2. Documents filed by companies with many federal regulatory authorities, such as the Federal Trade Commission, the Federal Communications Commission, the Consumer Product Safety Commission and the Environmental Protection Agency. In addition, these regulatory agencies produce documents that are almost always public record, and they often have complaints filed by consumers and businesses against companies they regulate.

    Please note that there are at least two documents with federal government agencies that a journalist might want that are **NOT** public record and not available to business reporters. These are initial complaints of harassment or discrimination filed with the Equal Employment Opportunity Commission and information that a pharmaceutical company supplies to the Food and Drug Administration when asking the FDA for approval to sell a drug to consumers.

    Also, proprietary information or trade secrets filed by companies with federal agencies could be exempt from being produced by the agency pursuant to a Freedom of Information Act request under Exemption 4, which protects confidential business information. For instance, there may be trade secret information in a patent application filed with the U.S. Patent and Trademark Office.

3. State documents, such as information about a company filed with the Secretary of State's Office and information with state regulatory agencies, such as the insurance department.

4. Lawsuits filed in both state and federal courts. These documents include initial complaints, affidavits, exhibits and depositions. Sometimes, lawsuits are sealed by companies that want to keep certain disclosures from the public, such as trade secrets. When a lawsuit is settled out of court, a confidential settlement is not a public record. The court record will simply indicate a dismissal. In addition, the parties to the litigation might sign an agreement of confidentiality that prohibits each side from making the terms of the settlement public — that happens all the time.

5. Form 990 filings by nonprofit organizations and foundations with the Internal Revenue Service.

6. State and federal government contracts with public and private companies.

7. Bankruptcy court filings for both individuals and businesses. These include lists of creditors, which often include their mailing address and phone numbers.

8. Real estate records such as the buying and selling of property and the rezoning of property for new uses. These records are kept at the municipal and county level.

Media organizations such as The New York Times, Bloomberg News and Fox Business Network filed lawsuits in 2008 and 2009 against the federal government, seeking access to records for the government's Troubled Asset Relief Program, or TARP, to gain access to details of financial bailout. While some of these lawsuits have been successful, the federal government resisted releasing much of this information.

Regulation Fair Disclosure

On Aug. 15, 2000, the Securities and Exchange Commission adopted Regulation Fair Disclosure to outlaw the selective disclosure of information by publicly traded companies and other issuers. Regulation FD provides that when an issuer discloses material nonpublic information to certain individuals or entities — generally, securities market professionals such as stock analysts or holders of the issuer's securities who may well trade on the basis of the information — the issuer must make public disclosure of that information. In this way, the new rule aims to promote the full and fair disclosure.

The full regulation can be read at: http://www.sec.gov/rules/final/33-7881. htm

In addition to helping investors, Regulation FD has been a boon to business journalism because it requires companies to provide access to its earnings conference calls and video conferences of investor presentations, among other events, to everyone, including reporters and editors who previously were not allowed to hear these calls. In fact, many business journalists argued in favor of

Regulation FD before it became a rule for this and other reasons.

Companies typically provide the access by releasing information about a conference call at the end of a news release, or by posting the information on its website. In many cases, a company will post a link to a video conference on its site as well.

The Securities and Exchange Commission staff has also recently decided that disseminating information on company websites is also considered a way to comply with Regulation FD. This includes blogging by chief executive officers and other executives. See further details here: http://www.sec.gov/news/speech/2008/spch073008km.htm

What all of this means is that a business journalist should be aware of Regulation Fair Disclosure and how it now requires companies to provide information.

In addition, Regulation FD has been interpreted as not preventing journalists from obtaining scoops and exclusives from companies.

Sourcing

Increasingly, business journalists are under threat to divulge their sources for stories as companies want to know where information was obtained.

Journalists are also potentially liable if they divulge where they obtained information if the informant had a binding oral contract with the reporter not to have his or her identity disclosed.

In the case of *Cohen v. Cowles Media,* a campaign adviser who acted as a source for a story about a politician running for governor had his name used in a Minneapolis Star Tribune story even though the reporter had promised not to identify the source. The editor included the information against the reporter's wishes, and the source lost his job. The source sued the newspaper for breaching the reporter's promise and won a substantial jury verdict in 1988 that ultimately was upheld by the U.S. Supreme Court in 1991.

A business journalist, as well as a confidential source, needs to understand precisely what deal is being cut. In most cases, the deal needs to be defined as narrowly as possible. Many journalists tell a source, "I will keep your name out of the paper." Reporters should also refrain from — or be very cautious about — promising a source that "no one will be able to identify you," as that usually cannot be guaranteed. Instead, the reporter and source might agree that the source will identified as, say, a "high-ranking corporate official."

Business journalists and their sources should also be comfortable with the terms "off the record" and "on background." They should reach an agreement as to whether that means the information can be used in a story without being attributed to the source.

In addition, business journalists could be subpoenaed by readers or investors to force disclosure of their sources. A growing controversy in business journalism centers on the use of hedge fund managers as sources and the relationship between business journalists and short sellers, but this issue has been ongoing for more than three decades.

In 1977, a class-action lawsuit was brought against Barron's columnist Alan Abelson, his editor and parent company Dow Jones & Co. The lawsuit, which was later dismissed, questioned whether Abelson was using short sellers as sources for his stories, with the short sellers knowing that Abelson would write a negative article about the stock mentioned by the investors.

The charges were never proved. In fact, Abelson had sued BusinessWeek magazine in 1975 after it published an article alleging that the Barron's writer leaked information to investors about his column. BusinessWeek subsequently disclaimed the story and admitted that it had "no evidence that advance information on the contents of Barron's was intentionally leaked to investors by Abelson, Barron's, or Dow Jones."

Although it is a broader issue, reporters subpoenaed in state proceedings to reveal a source (i.e., subpoenaed to testify in a criminal or civil case) might or might not have statutory protection. That would depend on whether the state in which the proceedings are pending has a shield statute and, if it does, what the terms of the statute are.

If the reporter is subpoenaed in a federal proceeding in which state law is not being applied, then the reporter will not have statutory protection because there is no federal shield law — although the reporter might have some degree of First Amendment protection depending on the circumstances and facts and on the U.S. Circuit in which the proceedings are pending. The U.S. Supreme Court has never implicitly recognized a First Amendment right of reporters to refuse to testify when subpoenaed in a lawfully convened civil or criminal proceeding.

International law

Finally, any business journalist should be aware that international law is different when it comes to the media and their reporting about companies. In addition, although a company or a CEO of a company is based in the United States, a company could file a claim in another country claiming the foreign courts have jurisdiction over the matter because the company has a reputation in that country and transacts business in that country, where the laws are less friendly to media organizations.

The Wall Street Journal has, for example, been a defendant in the Singapore judicial system in recent years. In March 2009, the paper was ruled in contempt and fined a small amount for two editorials and a letter to the editor it published about the country's judiciary system. In November 2008, Singapore's high court found an editor of The Journal in contempt of court and issued a fine for damaging the reputation of its judiciary relating to the same items.

There's also increasing pressure by some countries in the Middle East and Asia to prevent publishing information by business media outlets that might negatively affect the economy.

III. BUSINESS JOURNALISM GUIDELINES AND ETHICS

Not all aspects of business journalism are as cut and dried as the laws and rules that determine the release of information. That's why we're including this section on business journalism ethics.

There are no set guidelines in business journalism. Although many business journalists agree on certain issues, such as that trading in stocks of companies they report about is unethical, there are just as many other issues on which there is disagreement.

We're providing two sets of guidelines and ethical statements from two business media outlets — American City Business Journals and Bloomberg Businessweek — as recommended reading for any business journalist faced with an ethical issue.

Others can be found here:

1. Dow Jones Code of Ethics: http://www.dj.com/TheCompany/CodeConduct.htm
2. Thomson Reuters Code of Ethics: http://www.thomsonreuters.com/content/PDF/corporate/corp_govern/TR_COBC_English_20081028.pdf
3. American Business Media Code of Ethics: http://www.americanbusinessmedia.com/images/abm/pdfs/committees/EdEthics.pdf
4. American Society of Business Publication Editors Guide to Preferred Editorial Practices: http://www.asbpe.org/about/code.htm
5. Associated Press Statement of News Values and Principles: http://www.ap.org/newsvalues/index.html
6. Society of American Business Editors and Writers Code of Ethics: http://www.sabew.org/ethics/RevisedCodeofEthics.htm

When in doubt, however, let us emphasize that the best policy is to discuss the matter with your superior, or the editor-in-chief, before taking any action. An after-the-fact discussion won't undo any harm that might arise from your actions.

a. American City Business Journals Conflict of Interest Policy

This policy statement is designed to provide all employees with guidelines which will enable them to avoid conflicts of interest that might be construed to be detrimental to the best interests of ACBJ. It is important for all employees to keep in mind the tremendous embarrassment and damage to the Company's reputation and that of fellow employees that could come about through a lapse in judgment by one person, or someone closely associated with that person, no matter how well-intended that person may be. Because we think it is essential that every employee be above suspicion, we consider any slip in judgment in the areas covered in this policy statement to be serious enough to warrant dismissal.

Confidential Information

Employees should not use, directly or indirectly, for their own or any other person's financial gain, any information about ACBJ which the employee obtained in connection with ACBJ employment. Further, employees should not disclose to anyone confidential information obtained in connection with ACBJ.

Gifts, Purchases of Goods or Political Contributions

Employees should not requisition, order, approve or otherwise participate in the purchase of goods or services on behalf of ACBJ from any company in which the employee or a family member has any financial interest, whether stock ownership or loans or otherwise.

Employees should not accept, directly or indirectly, any gift, entertainment or reimbursement of expenses of more than twenty dollars or that exceeds customary courtesies, nor should they accept, directly or indirectly, payment, loan, services, employment or any other benefit from any company or individual that furnishes or seeks to furnish news, material, equipment, supplies or services to ACBJ.

Employees are not permitted to accept free transportation or lodging ("so-called junkets") offered by companies, individuals or governmental agencies.

Employees should not offer to provide, directly or indirectly, any gift, entertainment or reimbursement of expenses for more than nominal value or that exceeds customary courtesies, nor should they offer, directly or indirectly, any material, equipment or services to any company or person in position to make or influence any business or governmental decision affecting ACBJ.

ACBJ does not contribute directly or indirectly to political campaigns or to political parties or groups seeking to raise money for political parties or political campaigns, and ACBJ does not and will not reimburse any employee for any political contribution made by an employee.

Security Transactions

ACBJ has a strict policy on security transactions by employees who have access to inside information regarding unpublished stories or advertising schedules. It also has a strict related policy on the conduct of news and advertising staff members dealing with corporations we cover or whose advertising we carry. Each employee is expected to bend over backwards to avoid any action, no matter how well-intentioned, that could provide grounds even for suspicion:

(i) that an employee, his family or others close to the employee made financial gains by acting on the basis of "inside" information obtained through a position on our staff, before it was available to the general public. Such information includes hold-for-release material, our plans for running stories, items that may affect price movements, or projected advertising campaigns;

(ii) that an employee is financially committed in the market so deeply or in such other ways as to create a temptation to biased writing or scheduling of advertising;

(iii) that an employee is beholden to brokers or any other group we cover or advertisers. Such indebtedness could arise through acceptance of favors, gifts or payments for performing writing assignments or other services for them.

We do not want to penalize our staff members by suggesting that they not buy stocks or make other investments. We do, however, want employees to avoid speculation or the appearance of speculation. We reiterate that it is not enough to be incorruptible and act with honest motives. It is equally important to use good judgment and conduct one's outside activities so that no one — management, our editors, an SEC investigator, or a political critic of the Company — has any grounds for even raising the suspicion that an employee misused a position with the Company.

With these general propositions in mind, here are some further specific guidelines:

(i) First and foremost, all material gleaned by you in the course of your work for ACBJ is deemed to be strictly the Company's property. This includes not only the fruits of your own and your colleagues' work, but also information on plans for running items and articles on particular companies and industries and advertising schedules in future issues. Such material must never be disclosed to anyone outside of the Company, including friends and relatives. Viewing information as the Company's property should avoid a great many of the obvious pitfalls.

(ii) No employee regularly assigned to a specific industry should invest, nor should his family, in any company engaged in whole or significant part in that industry.

Serving on the Board of Directors of Other Companies

ACBJ employees are prohibited except with written approval of the chief executive officer from serving as directors or officers of any other company devoted to profit-making. Employees may not receive payment for serving on a board which is not devoted to making a profit. If an employee is involved in a family-owned profit-making business, clearance should be obtained in advance from the chief executive officer. If an employee's participation on a board of directors, of either a profit-making or nonprofit organization, creates the appearance of a potential conflict of interest with the company or a conflict of the editorial integrity of the newspaper, that person may be required by the chief executive officer to resign from that board of directors.

Accounting Procedures

No ACBJ fund, asset or liability which is not fully and properly recorded on the books and records shall be created or permitted to exist.

All employees will comply with ACBJ's accounting principles, procedures and controls and no false, artificial or misleading entries in our books and records shall be made for any reason whatsoever.

No ACBJ employee will:

(a) issue or authorize any official company document that is false or misleading;

(b) knowingly accept and treat as accurate a false or misleading document prepared by a person outside ACBJ; and

(c) knowingly make false or misleading statements to our external, internal or other auditors.

Only those corporate managers authorized to do so may release information regarding ACBJ. Management of individual papers may release information pertaining solely to their own market as outlined in the Company's policy manual.

We believe these guidelines should be easily understood. They aren't intended to deter any employee from participating actively in civic or charitable organization, provided they have no impact on or connection with ACBJ.

The same applies to political organization or government advisory boards for the average employee — but editorial employees and company executives would be expected to refrain if there were a connection with issues covered by his or her publication or if his or her superior didn't provide prior clearance.

We would like to emphasize that we have complete confidence in all of our employees. It is essential, however, that all of us maintain the highest standards of ethics in the conduct of ACBJ business in actuality and also in appearances by acting within the framework of these guidelines. Please retain this policy statement in your files.

Every ACBJ employee will be given a copy of this Conflict of Interest policy annually and acknowledge by signature that they understand and abide by it. All new employees will receive the policy at the time of hiring and acknowledge same.

Your cooperation is greatly appreciated.

b. The BusinessWeek Code of Journalistic Ethics

The code was last updated online on December 2, 2009. It is an abridged version of the document BusinessWeek journalists are required to sign annually.

What We Stand For

In our society, the press enjoys a remarkable degree of freedom. With that freedom comes the responsibility to practice our craft in accordance with the highest standards, to be accountable for what we publish, and to avoid conflicts of interest.

Ever since BusinessWeek was established in September, 1929, we have striven to fulfill these responsibilities. And with good reason. Otherwise, we could lose our most important asset: the trust of our readers, online visitors, viewers, and listeners in the credibility of the information and insights we provide.

We believe that our future depends upon preserving and enhancing this trust. Therefore, we must ensure that:

1. The integrity of our journalists is of the highest caliber.
2. We base our unique brand of journalism on accurate information, gathered honestly and presented fairly.
3. Our journalists' professional conduct is unassailable.
4. Our journalists' personal conduct, as it reflects on BusinessWeek, is beyond reproach.

All members of the BusinessWeek editorial staffs must uphold these principles. This means everyone who works on the magazine, the Web site, or in our multimedia operations (including members of the art, production, and systems departments, all Web developers and programmers, and all assistants and clerical workers), be they full-time, part-time, interns, or freelancers.

Here are the rules by which they must live:

INTEGRITY

1. "Church and State."

Unquestionable integrity is at the heart of BusinessWeek's effort to serve our audiences with the best business journalism in the world. One way we achieve this is to strictly observe an invisible wall that separates our editorial operations from our advertising and other business departments, so as to avoid any chance that one will inappropriately influence the other.

In every medium, our reporters, editors, and producers prepare and place stories, graphics, and interactive features based solely on their editorial merits. Thus, we treat companies that advertise with us exactly the same as those that don't. We don't favor any company or subject of a story, or discriminate against any — for any reason.

Moreover, editors and editorial imperatives dictate the design of our products. Obviously, we make allowance for the presentation of revenue-generating elements. However, the design must always make clear the distinction between editorial and commercial material. In the spirit of that rule, for example, we do not link, for any reason other than editorial purposes, from within the text of electronic versions of our stories to an advertiser's Web site.

2. ASME guidelines.

The American Society of Magazine Editors has created guidelines for both print and digital media that establish a minimum standard of behavior for reputable magazines and Web sites. BusinessWeek and its employees, both editorial and business, must honor the ASME guidelines. (Editorial Guidelines: http://www. magazine.org/Editorial/Guidelines/. Best Practices for Digital Media: http:// www.magazine.org/Editorial/Guidelines/Best_Practices_for_Digital_Media/). We will treat violations of them as violations of our journalistic ethics.

OUR JOURNALISTIC STANDARDS

BusinessWeek specializes in valued-added, interpretive journalism. This gives us license to go beyond a traditional, just-the-facts approach. At the same time, it puts an extra onus on us in the following areas:

1. **Accuracy.**

   For the reader to believe our interpretations, we must start with accurate information, honestly and professionally gathered. Moreover, our interpretation must flow from the facts and be reasonable.

   Inaccurate or sloppy reporting of material that appears anywhere under the BusinessWeek name violates the spirit of this Code. The responsibility for accuracy lies with everyone who touches the editorial product.

2. **Honesty.**

   All of our journalists' dealings with sources — and with other editorial staff — must be truthful.

   As an institution, moreover, BusinessWeek will always be an independent voice, with no ax to grind. We do not support political candidates or political parties. We are not Keynesians, monetarists, or supply-siders. On all matters of politics, economics, and social policy, we try to bring our own judgment to bear, based on thorough reporting and reasonable analysis. We do not do stories that are designed to hew to any ideological agenda.

3. **Fairness.**

We give the subjects of a story — people, companies, and institutions — an opportunity to have their views presented. We include relevant portions of those views — or report that the subject declines to comment. We also present differing or dissenting opinions, though they may be subordinate to the main thrust of the story.

If someone complains about a story, we will investigate promptly and even-handedly. If we are right, we will stand by the story regardless of who is complaining. If we are wrong, we will say so forthrightly and make whatever amends seem appropriate.

Because we do analytic journalism and commentaries, we do not strive for perfect objectivity. But we must always strive to be fair.

4. **Attribution.**

We use the following ground rules when seeking information from sources:
On the record:
Journalists are free to use all material from the interview, including information and quotations, and to identify the source. We prefer this approach.

Not for attribution:
Journalists are free to use information and quotations, but they agree not to identify the source. "Not for attribution" is an acceptable method of gathering information, though not the one we prefer.

Journalists generally should have more than one source for information that you can't attribute, both to double-check its veracity and to guard against being used or misled by a single source.

Off the record:
Journalist agrees not to use information from the source. Or journalist may agree not to use the information unless he/she checks with the source before publication. We ask our journalists to avoid this method unless it's the only way to interview a one-of-a-kind source.

Routine attribution:
"He said" means the journalist got the quote from the source -- in person, at a press conference, or on the phone. "He said in a statement" or "in a report" means the quote came from a written statement or press release, or from a document such as an analyst's report. "He said in an e-mail interview" means exactly that. If the quote comes from another news outlet, the journalist must credit it: "President Smith told the Associated Press."